SESSIONS WITH JOHN

Smyth & Helwys Publishing, Inc.
6316 Peake Road
Macon, Georgia 31210-3960
1-800-747-3016

Library of Congress Cataloging-in-Publication Data

Setzer, Robert B., Jr.

Sessions with John: The Vocabulary of Grace / by Robert B. Setzer, Jr.
p. cm.
Includes bibliographical references and index.
ISBN 978-1-57312-560-4 (pbk. : alk. paper)
1. Bible. N.T. John—Textbooks. I. Title.
BS2616.S47 2010
226.5'06—dc22

2010018467

Sessions *with* John

The *Vocabulary* of *Grace*

Robert B. Setzer, Jr.

Also by Robert B. Setzer, Jr.

Christianity for Beginners

Encounters with the Living Christ: Meeting Jesus in the Gospel of John

Dedication

To the good people of the First Baptist Church of Christ of Macon, Georgia,
who taught me far more about knowing, loving, and
following Jesus than I ever taught them.

And to Bambi—
my wife, pastor, and friend—
who has become Christ's truth and grace to me time and time again.

Table of Contents

Introduction

The Spiral Staircase of John's Gospel

For reasons no one really knows, William Sherman spared my fair city of Macon, Georgia, during his infamous march to the sea. Some say Sherman was running low on ammo. Some say he was in a rush to get to Savannah by Christmas. Whatever the reason, because the good general skirted Macon rather than sacking it, this quaint city in Middle Georgia is home to some of the finest antebellum homes in the state.

One of those homes, the Oliver House at 1183 Georgia Avenue, sits on a prominent corner on College Hill, not far from the First Baptist Church of Christ where I serve as pastor. Recently, I visited this Greek Revival home built in 1848 and was dazzled by what I saw. Upon entering the foyer, one is met by a stunningly beautiful spiral staircase that ascends an octagonal hall. The staircase lifts the eye to a medallion in the ceiling, three floors above, from which hangs an ornate and lovely chandelier that descends to the foyer below.

The enchanting power of a spiral staircase rests in its ability to provide an ever-changing perspective on the same space. As one ascends the staircase, the sights above and below are seen again and again, but each time from a slightly different angle, at varying distances, and in shifting light. The result is a much fuller immersion in the beauty of a lovely, inviting entrance than is possible from ordinary stairs.

Think of the Gospel of John as a spiral staircase. In John's story of Jesus, certain words, images, and themes appear again and again. The reader leaves a given emphasis only to circle around and see it reappear, but this time in a different context. With each "spiral" of the truth or theme, the reader's grasp of the message deepens until

Jesus' "words of life" penetrate the deepest parts of the self where real transformation begins (6:63, 68; unless otherwise indicated, all translations are from the NRSV).

Take, for example, the theme of "light" in John's Gospel. Light appears at the very beginning of John's Gospel where we learn that the eternal Word of God, namely Jesus, is the "light shining in the darkness" (1:4-5, 9). However, a grave spiritual crisis exists because so many prefer the darkness of their self-deception and sin to the light of God's new day dawning in Jesus (3:19-21). Jesus comes to shatter the world's darkness with the light of God's unfailing truth and love, boldly declaring himself "the light of the world" (8:12a; 9:5). Those who follow him will no longer "walk in darkness" but have "the light of life" (8:12b; 1:4-5). This riveting possibility is then given dramatic expression in the story of the man born blind whom Jesus restores to sight, both physically and spiritually. As a result, this once-blind man is freed to live a bolder, more beautiful life than he ever thought possible (ch. 9).

This sort of meandering round and round—touching on a theme, leaving it, and then revisiting it—is typical of John's Gospel. Because of that, this book, *Sessions with John: The Vocabulary of Grace*, is organized thematically rather than proceeding verse by verse, chapter by chapter. Each session of this book traces a single word or theme throughout the Gospel. In that way, readers can view the whole of a given truth as it develops, step by step, up each round of a spiraling ascent toward ever clearer, life-changing truth.

The words and themes chosen for this study of John's Gospel are "word and flesh," "light," "signs," "born again," "believe," "truth," "eternal life," "love," "Paraclete," "abide," "glorified," "Lamb of God," "blessed," and "bread and fish." Certainly, this list is not exhaustive; in a longer work, other words might be added. However, the keys words in this study provide an ample introduction to the major themes and movements of John's Gospel.

The purpose for which John's Gospel was written, after all, was not comprehensive *knowledge* (20:30) but comprehensive *transformation* (20:31): becoming a new person by trusting in and following Jesus (3:16; 8:12). Thus, the word and thematic studies at the heart of *Sessions with John: The Vocabulary of Grace* are meant to offer Jesus' "words of life" to a new generation of believers. Those who prayerfully ponder and strive to live these words—in the power of Jesus' own risen life (15:4-5)—will discover these words yet have power to breathe God's peace and presence into every believing heart. Such truths then become and will forever remain a precious part of one's "vocabulary of grace" (1:16).

Author and Purpose of John's Gospel

The author of John's Gospel does not identify himself by name. He calls himself only "the beloved disciple," a somewhat mysterious figure who appears throughout the Gospel (13:23; 19:26-27, 35; 20:2-8; 21:7, 20-24). From these references, we can see the beloved disciple was one of the twelve disciples; he reclined next to Jesus at the Last Supper, and from the cross, Jesus entrusted the care of his mother to this disciple.

The title, "The Gospel according to John," was not part of the original Gospel but was added in the second century. That title reflects the consensus of the early church that the beloved disciple was John, the son of Zebedee and brother of James (Mark 1:19-20; 3:17). During the ministry of Jesus, this John belonged to Jesus' inner circle of Peter, James, and John (Mark 9:2; 14:33).

The Gospel of John was likely drawn from the eyewitness account of the Apostle John. The author of this Gospel shows an eyewitness's recall for detail, noting for example the *boy* in the crowd who brought Jesus *barley* loaves (6:9), describing the blood and water that gushed from Jesus' side on the cross (19:34-35), and noting the state of Jesus' grave clothes (20:6b-7). These revealing observations are omitted in the other Gospels.

However, many interpreters believe John's Gospel was put in its final form by someone highly trained in Greek language and philosophy like that reflected in the Prologue to the Gospel (1:1-18). Indeed, at the close of John's Gospel, we read, "This is the disciple who is testifying to these things and has written them, and *we know* that his testimony is true" (21:24, italics mine; see also 3:11). The "we" of such passages probably points to the believing community that gathered around John and helped record and polish his witness.

Putting all the puzzle pieces together, perhaps the most likely scenario is this: the Apostle John settled in Ephesus and became a renowned Christian leader in Asia Minor. While there, he—and/or a gifted disciple of his—completed the masterpiece we know today as the Gospel of John. This author probably also produced the Letters of John in the New Testament.

Regardless of the definite authorship, the authority of John's Gospel is not based in knowing the exact identity of the author—who, again, is never named—but in the power of this remarkable book to achieve its purpose: "these [things] are written so that you may come to believe that Jesus is the Messiah, the Son of God, and that through believing you may have life in his name" (20:31).

Interestingly, the author of John was far less interested in promoting himself than his message. Perhaps that's why Jesus considered him "beloved"!

As to the specific circumstances that evoked John's witness, the Gospel itself suggests Christians in Asia Minor were facing ridicule, rejection, and persecution (9:22; 12:42; 16:2; 20:19). Much of this struggle arose from the deepening Christian/Jewish rift that followed the destruction of the temple in AD 70. Sadly, because John sometimes speaks of "the Jews" in angry, accusing ways, the charge has been leveled that John's Gospel is anti-Semitic. Such a charge is unfounded. John recognizes that Jesus was a Jew, as were all of his disciples and many others who believed in him and followed him, as reported by John's own witness (8:30-31; 10:19-21; 11:45; 12:11).

For John, the expression "the Jews" usually means the religious establishment opposing Jesus. The phrase should be read as expressive of the tensions in that time and place and not as an indictment of Jews generally. All believers facing persecution from whatever source can count on the Advocate, the Holy Spirit, to encourage and embolden them (16:1-4; 9:25, 30-33).

Beyond its immediate audience of persecuted believers, John's Gospel is addressed to the wider world (1:29; 3:16), especially the Gentile or Greek-speaking world to which his poetic and philosophical Prologue is addressed (1:1-18; see also 12:20-24). Jesus has come not just to "the Jews" (4:21-23) but to all who will receive him and, in receiving him, will be reborn as sons and daughters of God (1:11-12).

For people of every race, class, and creed, John's powerful, evocative witness has worked its magic. Because of the immortal words spoken and penned by this gifted Evangelist, countless believers have celebrated and lived the confession, "It is no longer because of what you said that we believe, for we have heard for ourselves, and we know that this is truly the Savior of the world" (4:42).

The Unique Character of John's Gospel

Even casual readers of the Gospels soon recognize that John is different in tone and feel from the other three. Indeed, the first three Gospels are called the "Synoptic Gospels," from a Greek expression meaning "to see alike." Matthew, Mark, and Luke tell a similar story and share a great deal of material. The fourth Gospel charts a different path and speaks with a different voice.

Here are a few of the more striking contrasts between John and the Synoptics: the Synoptics feature the parables of Jesus, while in John's Gospel, Jesus gives long, philosophical speeches. The Synoptics are filled with the miracles of Jesus, while the fourth Gospel details only seven stately "signs." Exorcisms abound in the Synoptics but are altogether lacking in John. Key events from Jesus' life in the Synoptics, such as his birth, wilderness temptations, the Transfiguration, the confession at Caesarea-Philippi, and Jesus' prayer in Gethsemane, are completely missing in John. Finally, John includes riveting stories like the woman at the well (ch. 4), the woman caught in adultery (ch. 8), and the raising of Lazarus (ch. 11), which the Synoptics don't mention at all.

Why is John's witness so different from the other three? One early and helpful answer was suggested by the church father, Clement of Alexandria. Writing about 200 BC, he observed that "John, last of all, conscious that the outward facts had been set forth in the Gospels, was urged on by his disciples, and, divinely moved by the Spirit, composed a *spiritual* Gospel." That is an apt way to describe the difference between John and the Synoptics. John is more "spiritual." John seems to assume his readers "know the facts," so he goes behind the facts to give a deeper sense of meaning. John is more given to symbolism and metaphor, more inclined to peek behind the curtain and tell us what is going on backstage.

In addition, John's Gospel is widely believed to be the last of the four Gospels written, coming into its final form late in the first century. If indeed the disciple John wrote this Gospel, as the early church believed, he did so at an advanced age. As such, his Gospel reflects a mature and profound theological reflection on the person and work of Jesus.

In John's Gospel, Jesus promises to return in the power of the Holy Spirit to instruct his church (14:26). Indeed, Jesus needs and wants to say many things to his disciples, but they "cannot bear them now" (16:12). In the searing light of Jesus' Easter triumph, a much fuller revelation of his glory will come into focus (2:22; 20:9). That's when the "Spirit of truth" will come to "guide [them] into all the truth" (16:13).

When Jesus speaks in John's Gospel, he speaks as both the earthly Jesus (1:14, 18) and the risen Lord (16:14-15), ever deepening the insight of John and his church into the wonder of God's descent into the world in Jesus Christ. It is not possible or necessary to distinguish between the actual sayings of the historical Jesus and the biblical truth bequeathed to us by the risen Christ. In all events, his word is God's truth to us. His word is life (6:63b, 68). His words form the heart of the believer's "vocabulary of grace."

The fact that John's Gospel found its place in the canon alongside the other three indicates that the first Christians heard in its witness the unmistakable voice of their Lord (20:28) and Savior (4:42). Those who continue to open themselves to John's witness find that the Risen One still honors his promise not to leave his beloved ones orphaned (14:18). Again and again, in the power of his word and Spirit, he is present at their side.

John the Eagle

The style and content of John's Gospel is markedly different from the first three Gospels, but that is due to the time and place of his witness and the purpose for which he wrote. This Gospel certainly deserves and has won a treasured place in many hearts. Indeed, for many Christians, no book of the Bible is more beloved, or read with greater devotion, than the Gospel of John.

Augustine likened the Gospel of John to the eagle because the eagle alone could look into the sun and not be blinded. Likewise, John looks directly into the glory of God in the face of Jesus Christ (2 Cor 4:6). By God's grace, he lives to tell the tale, and all who read his witness are blessed.

Yes, the Gospel of John loops and ascends like a spiral staircase. But when it works its magic, we take flight from the top step and soar upward like an eagle until we look into the very face of God (1:18).

1. Search the Internet for "images spiral staircase" and ponder some of the photos you see. Why are spiral staircases so magical and inviting? Can you remember a time when you stood upon a beautiful spiral staircase?

____

____

____

____

____

2. Does the thematic approach of this book—and John's Gospel—appeal to you? Why or why not?

____

____

____

____

____

3. Which of the four Gospels is your favorite? Why?

____

____

____

____

____

4. Flip through the Gospel of John and look for highlights. What are your favorite stories from this Gospel? Your favorite verses?

____

____

____

____

____

5. Besides the key words treated in this study (see table of contents), what other words belong to your personal "vocabulary of grace"?

6. What metaphors suggest the difference between John and the Synoptics (for example, a realistic painting versus an impressionistic one; a news article versus the editorial page)?

7. What questions about John's Gospel do you bring to this study? What questions about Jesus do you bring to this study?

Session 1

Word and Flesh

John 1:1-18

When it comes to Christmas, everything we know about the subject, biblically speaking, comes from Matthew and Luke. Mark, always in a hurry, races past the story of Jesus' birth. In Mark's Gospel, Jesus bursts on the scene fully grown and begins his ministry without prelude or prologue.

Matthew and Luke move at a more leisurely pace. Their material reads like a Hallmark classic. They tell a quaint story of angels, shepherds, and wise men.

When John takes up the tale, he pans the camera back across untold eons to the very beginning of time. What do we see way back then besides Jesus and God, already joined in a dance of holy love?

Imagine a film based on the opening verses of John's Gospel. The usual Christmas pageant fare of shepherds dressed in bathrobes and wise men toting shoe boxes simply wouldn't do. Instead, we might begin with a brilliant quasar lighting up the dark recesses of deepest space. From that celestial glory, 30,000 times brighter than our Milky Way, a silvery ray of light starts hurtling through space.

Streaking across the night sky, the light travels from the farthest rim of the universe toward a tiny blue-green ball called planet earth. Upon entering Andromeda, the streak of light begins reeling itself in, as the captain of a sailing vessel might furl his sails. The light balls itself up tighter and tighter, until it is smaller than the finest pinprick of a white hot laser. Entering earth's atmosphere, the fiery dot becomes smaller still, so small it can pierce a virgin's womb without her knowing she has been touched by holy light.

Riding the wings of Israel's hopes and prayers for a thousand years, the brilliant speck of light homes in on the hill country of Palestine. Within the universe of a peasant's womb, it searches for the egg as it searched for the earth before. When it finds the egg and wraps it in divine radiance, a miracle happens.

As in the beginning, God called forth the world from nothingness, so from the nothingness of a virgin's womb, God calls forth his Son. *"And the word became flesh, and dwelt among us"* (v. 14). In that simple yet stupendous phrase, John tells us a riveting, world-altering truth: Jesus is the eternal Word and Son of God who has come to indwell a fully human life.

The Word

When John speaks of the "Word" who dwelt with God at the beginning (1:1), he uses the Greek word *logos*, a word rich in associations and meaning.

Among Jesus' own people, the Jews, the "word of God" was God's all-powerful self-expression. At the sound of God's word, "Let there be light!" the heavens and the earth leapt into being (Gen 1:3; Ps 33:6). God's divine word shaped not only creation, but also history, as God spoke to the chosen people, Israel, through the prophets (Amos 3:7-8). God's word sometimes brought rebuke (Amos 5:6-9) and sometimes hope and healing (Ps 107:19-20). In a richly evocative passage in Proverbs 8, the word of God is closely linked to the wisdom of God. Like the Logos in John 1, this Wisdom (*Sophia* in Greek) is cast as a woman present at creation (Prov 8:22-31).

Within the wider Greco-Roman world, the term "logos" or "word" was also significant. Stoic philosophers used the term to designate the cosmic reason undergirding the universe. In much Greek thinking, the logos referred to what today might be called "divine reason" or "the mind of God."

Thus, in claiming that in Jesus of Nazareth, the eternal and divine logos had fully indwelt a human life, John made a twofold claim: to Jews, he said, "If you want to see God's word in *action*, look to Jesus"; to Gentiles, steeped in the philosophical currents of their age, John said, "If you want to see the *order and meaning* at the heart of the cosmos, look to Jesus." It was and is a stunning claim: the decisive clue to Ultimate Reality is Jesus Christ.

The Nature of the Logos

In the opening verse of his Gospel, John says three essential things about the Logos: (1) the Logos was present at the beginning of creation; (2) the Logos was *with* God; (3) the Logos *was* God. As one might paraphrase the opening verse of John's Gospel, "*When* God was, the Word was; *where* God was, the Word was; *what* God was, the Word was" (Hull, 212).

The Logos, the Word, is eternal, belonging to the very nature and essence of God. While the Word *became* flesh (v. 14), from the very beginning the Word *was* God (v. 1). Never was there a time when God was without the Word. Yet this Word is not an object (an "it") but a Person ("he," vv. 2-4). The Word is identified with God ("*was* God") yet remains distinct from God ("*with* God").

This sort of mind-bending truth characterizes the Gospel of John. Those looking for a simplistic expression of faith will likely get frustrated. Those willing to let John's probing Gospel upset their conventional view of religious truth will be richly rewarded.

God's Re-creation of the World

As the One "with God" who "is God," present at the very beginning, the Word is the agent of creation (v. 3). As in the book of Genesis, heaven and earth come into being at the sound of God's all-creative word (Gen 1:3, 6, 9, and so on). But John reveals that Word was not an impersonal force but the eternal Son of God (vv. 14, 18). The eternal Christ as the one through whom God created the universe is a theme explored elsewhere in the New Testament (Col 1:16-17; Heb 1:1-2).

Unlike ancient Greek philosophy that held the world of matter was inherently evil, both Christians and Jews believe God created the world and, hence, the world is profoundly "good" (Gen 1:4, 10, 12, and so on)! As Archbishop William Temple reportedly observed, "God must love matter because he made an awful lot of it."

In fact, John 1:1-5 artfully mirrors the language and meaning of Genesis 1. Both Genesis and John begin with "In the beginning," and creation themes abound. At God's word (1:1; Gen 1:3), light bursts forth (1:3b; Gen 1:3b), and that light allows life to flourish in its wake (Gen 1:11, 20, 24, and so on; John 1:4b-5). Unlike John the Baptist—and other great prophets and teachers who *bore witness* to the light (1:7-8), Jesus *is* the light (8:12). He is the life-giving light of God's presence, truth, and love pouring into a world shrouded by darkness and death (1:5; 3:19).

The overwhelming truth of John 1:1-13 is that in Jesus Christ, the Word-made-flesh, God is re-creating the world. God loves the world (3:16) and is acting to reclaim and restore a fallen creation. Surely there is no one better able to restore the world's broken relationship with the Creator than the Logos who created the world in the first place! Yet ironically, the very agent of creation—the eternal Logos or Christ—will be rejected by many of God's would-be children (vv. 10-11). However, those who "receive" the Word, Jesus Christ, and "believe in his name" (v. 12) are spiritually reborn as the sons and daughters of God (vv. 12-13).

In John's Gospel, to "believe" is to "follow" and live in the light of Jesus Christ (8:12; 12:46) where new (3:3, 5), abundant (10:10), and eternal (3:16) life is found. More on that will follow later in this book. For now, we reach the climax of John's first eighteen verses, a passage often referred to as the "Prologue."

The Word Made Flesh

The climatic statement in John's Prologue and, indeed, in John's Gospel is v. 14: "And the Word *became flesh* and lived among us." Up to this point, much of what John has said is fairly conventional. In many ways, his Prologue sounds a lot like the personification of wisdom as *Sophia* found in Proverbs 8. Thus far, a first-century Stoic philosopher would contest little in John's Prologue. Some scholars even believe the lofty opening paragraphs of John's Gospel are adapted from a Greek or Jewish poem already in circulation.

But when John proclaims, "And the Word *became flesh*," he's on his own. The notion that the eternal logos—God's creative, all-powerful word—would take up residence in a Jewish carpenter from Nazareth was utterly without precedent. Indeed, it would have been unthinkable apart from the staggering impact Jesus had on those who knew and loved him; but when they looked into his eyes, they saw a light that shone brighter than all the constellations of the night, and in his face, shimmering with holy fire, they caught glimpses of God.

Even in English, the shock of the word lands like cold water splashed on the face: "And the Word became *flesh*." Not "and the Word became *a person*," but the "Word became *flesh*." In Greek, the language of the New Testament, the noise of alien worlds colliding is louder still: "And the Logos [the Word] became *sarx* [flesh]. " *Sarx* is a bitter, biting word, the root of our word *sarcasm*. For the Greeks, the body, the *flesh* was a contaminated holding tank for the eternal spirit. To elegant, refined Greeks, steeped in the exalted language of the *"logos,"* the notion of God becoming flesh was utterly scandalous. But John doesn't flinch at the word; indeed, he glories in it! "The Word *became* flesh" (v. 14).

A lot turns on "became." The Word didn't *don* our flesh like a costume; the Word didn't *use* our flesh like a canvas; no, the Word *became* a real flesh-and-blood person, through and through. The Word *became* the human nature he bore so that Jesus and the Word are one forevermore.

The true and full humanity of Jesus is at the heart of the New Testament confidence that God knows our hearts: "For we do not have a high priest who is unable to sympathize with our weaknesses, but we have one who *in every respect has been tested as we are,* yet without sin. Let us therefore approach the throne of grace with boldness" (Heb 4:15-16a, italics mine). Jesus means God knows our humanity not from detached observation like a scientist watching lab rats but from the inside out. As Clarence Jordan noted in a provocative comment, "The emphasis of the New Testament is not so much on the divinity of Jesus as on the humanity of God."

"The Word became flesh *and lived among us.*" The verb "lived" can be rendered more literally "pitched his tent" or "tabernacled" among us. Such language hearkens back to the exodus when God's glory was manifested in the "Tent of Meeting," a portable shrine that accompanied the Hebrews during their sojourn in the wilderness (Exodus 40:34-38; 25:8; 33:7-11). The Tent of Meeting or "tabernacle" shrouded God's glory sufficiently so that God's awesome presence and power did not overwhelm or destroy the people. So too in Jesus of Nazareth, the divine glory of God was manifest as the Logos "pitched his tent" among us or, as Eugene Peterson imaginatively paraphrases in *The Message*, "moved into the neighborhood with us."

"And we have *seen his glory*, the glory as of a *father's only son.*" Here John introduces the Father/Son language for God and Jesus so central to his Gospel. Indeed, at this point John leaves the title of the "Logos" behind and starts referring to Jesus with the more intimate language of God's *Son.* Yet John's artful use of the "Logos" language makes clear what his Gospel will say again and again: Jesus is the Son of God in a way that no one else is. He is the "only Son"; he alone is the Son of God in a cosmic and eternal sense (v. 18). What he was by nature—God's "only begotten Son" (3:16, KJV)—we can become through a spiritual rebirth: sons and daughters of God (vv. 12-13; John 3:3, 6).

"The *Word* became *flesh.*" That phrase holds the mystery at the heart of John's Gospel: Jesus is both fully divine ("the Word") and fully human ("flesh"). This stunning confession is the great divide, the distinctive truth that sets Christianity apart from every other religious or philosophical system. Unlike every other religious teacher, ancient and modern, in which God's truth becomes words and more words, in Jesus of Nazareth, God's truth, God's essence, God's glory becomes *flesh*—one of us. And that makes all the difference.

Several years ago during a breakout session at the annual meeting of the Cooperative Baptist Fellowship, I heard Bill Leonard speak about participating in a Christian-Muslim dialogue. Dr. Leonard, then dean of the Wake Forest Divinity School, was surprised at how much he and his Muslin counterpart held in common. Among other things, they shared a commitment to truth, social justice, and a holy vocation.

But then they came to the great divide: Jesus Christ. Said the Muslim holy man, "I simply can't believe in a God who would become human."

And Dr. Leonard answered, "And I can't believe in a God who wouldn't."

Grace upon Grace

Yes, the "Law"—God's truth—was "given through Moses" (v. 17a); but "grace *and* truth came through Jesus Christ" (v. 17b). The shocking, scandalous grace of God is known most fully in God's eternal Word and Son becoming a real, flesh-and-blood person, Jesus Christ. Clearly, this passionate, reckless God will stop at nothing in pursing lost and wayward children and awakening them to their true destiny. As the early church father, Irenaeus, said it, "He became what we are that we might become what he is": sons and daughters of God (v. 12).

John's claim for Jesus, "From his fullness we have all received grace upon grace" (v. 16), is also true of John's Gospel. As one ponders the stories and truths of "the Word made flesh" told in this masterful work, the wonder of what God has done in Jesus Christ begins to stir. In time, some will find themselves coming to believe, to trust in the Jesus who comes near in John's witness. Those who do will discover that the living God is yet able to create a whole new world through him: "For if anyone is *in Christ,* he or she is a new creation. The old has passed away; behold, the new has come!" (2 Cor 5:17).

1. In his use of the "Logos," John drew on an image common to both the Jewish and Greek worlds. Is today's church adept at expressing the gospel in terms the larger world can understand? Do you know a writer or thinker who is?

2. Is Jesus God's Son in a way no one else is? What about Jesus' life and experience were unique?

3. What are some ways one might "make flesh" the love of God? Can you relate an experience in which someone "fleshed out" the love of God for you in a very personal way?

4. At the end of John's Gospel, the risen Jesus appears with his crucifixion scars intact (20:24-29). What, if anything, does that suggest about the continuing "humanity of God"?

5. In what ways does Jesus bring "grace upon grace" (v. 6)? How is "grace upon grace" different from simply "grace"?

6. John says Jesus brings truth *and* grace (v. 17). What happens when grace dispenses with the truth? What happens when the truth is spoken without grace?

7. Do you agree that the confession of Jesus as the "word made flesh" is the "great divide" that distinguishes Christianity from other faiths? Why or why not?

8. How has Jesus "recreated" your world? How is your "world" different because of Jesus? What would you lack without him?

Session 2

Light

John 1:4-5, 9; 8:12; 9:1-41

The darkest dark I ever saw was in Mammoth Cave, Kentucky. After a long, winding trek into the bowels of the earth, the guide led us into a huge, cavernous chamber. Lamps the size of streetlights lit the clammy, cold cave, pumping hope into that forlorn, foreboding space. Then the guide warned he was going to douse the lights and that when he did, we would experience darkness like none we had known before.

Then he flipped a switch and I was swallowed by a black hole, utterly devoid of light. The darkness was suffocating, like plastic wrap pressed against the face. Even after my eyes adjusted, I could see no hint of my hand two inches from my face. No one doubted the guide when he told us a few days spent in such utter darkness would drive one stark, raving mad.

The darkness pressed harder and harder, squeezing its prey, until I knew someone—maybe *me*—would soon cry for relief. Just then, the guide struck a match. The sound of that match and the brilliant, piercing light that sprung from its tip calmed my trembling heart. It was as though lurking demons, emboldened by the darkness, were beaten back by that single, pinprick of fire. Hungrily, greedily, I devoured that light. Never before had the words from John's Gospel struck with such visceral force: "And the light shines in the darkness and the darkness [*Thank God!*] cannot extinguish it!" (1:5).

The Light Shines in the Darkness

That's the stunning power and promise of Jesus Christ: he is the light shining *in* the darkness. In this broken world where we live, his is not a light that banishes the darkness like sunrise chasing away the night. Such a blazing revelation of Jesus' light must await our seeing him face to face and gazing in wonder at the fullness of his glory (1 John 3:1-2; 1 Cor 13:12). But for now, the light of Jesus Christ is the light shining *in* the darkness because that is where we live: in the darkness of our unbelief, the darkness of our dogged doubts and crippling fears, and yes, the darkness of our sin.

The stark contrast between light and dark is a fixture of John's Gospel and of the New Testament letters that bear his name: 1, 2, and 3 John: "God is light and in God there is no darkness at all" (1 John 1:5). In John 12:46, Jesus declares, "I have come as light into the world, so that everyone who believes in me should not remain in the darkness." Perhaps the most vivid contrast between light and dark in John's Gospel is in chapter 3: "And this is the judgment, that the light has come into the world, and people loved darkness rather than light because their deeds were evil" (3:19).

Thus, Nicodemus comes to Jesus "by night" (3:2). In this highly symbolic Gospel, Nicodemus is moving toward Jesus' light from the darkness of his disbelief. Similarly, the disciples are "in the dark" while crossing the Sea of Galilee because "Jesus had not yet come to them" (6:17). Later, after Jesus washes the disciples' feet, Judas leaves to perform his dastardly deed, and John's Gospel notes ominously, "And it was night" (13:30). In the other Gospels, the women come to the empty tomb at first light, but in John's Gospel, Mary Magdalene comes to the tomb "while it was still dark" (20:1).

In contrast to the creation story in Genesis, where one can view light and dark as complementary realities (Gen 1:5), in John's Gospel, darkness is viewed as inherently evil. It is the place of unbelief in and disobedience to the light of God in Jesus Christ (8:12). Since life can flourish only where there is light (1:4), the darkness is a place of spiritual despair and death (3:16).

The Darkness Cannot Extinguish the Light

Yet no matter how thick or impenetrable the darkness, Jesus is the light shining *in* the darkness. The greatness of any light is directly proportional to the depth of the darkness. Outside at noon, a match's light is negligible, but in a home plunged into pitch blackness by a nighttime power outage—where young children cry in terror—the light of that same match is priceless.

The wonderful thing about Jesus is that no matter how dark our doubt and disobedience, the light of God's light and truth shimmering in and through him is brighter still. John's Gospel confidently asserts, "The light shines in the darkness, and the darkness did not *overcome* it" (v. 5, italics mine). The Greek word translated "overcome" in the New Revised Standard Version of the Bible can also mean "understand" or "comprehend," as in the New International and King James versions of the Bible. John may well intend the double meaning: (1) the world of sin and darkness cannot *fathom* God's extravagant love in Jesus Christ, but (2) neither can that world *extinguish* the light of God in him. The light of Jesus Christ shines defiantly *in* the darkness; his is the "true light" that "enlightens everyone," whether he or she welcomes the light or not (vv. 9-11).

The light of friendship, it is said, is like the light of phosphorous. It shines brightest when all around is dark. As John's Gospel will reveal, that is truer of no one more than Jesus.

The Light of the World

Twice in John's Gospel, Jesus declares himself the "light of the world" (8:12; 9:5). It is a bold, all-encompassing statement. To be the source of light is to be the source of life, and John's Jesus intends to claim nothing less. As Jesus says in John 8:12, "Whoever follows me will never walk in darkness but will have *the light of life*." Jesus gives the "light of life" because in his light, life *abundant* (1:3-4; 10:10) and life *eternal* (3:15-16; 5:39; 10:28; 17:3) are found.

In Kathleen Norris's spiritual memoir, *A Cloister Walk*, she notes that the Greek word *photismos* is an ancient word for baptism (New York: Riverhead Books, 1996). That word shares a root with our word "photosynthesis," the process by which leaves turn light into life. Likewise, in our baptism, we come to life as we leave the darkness of our unbelief to live ever more fully in the light of God's gracious, forgiving love in Jesus Christ.

The Man Born Blind

The story of the man born blind in John 9 shows how Jesus transforms those who live in the bright, life-giving light of his presence. The story begins as Jesus leaves the temple (8:59), where for nearly two chapters of John's Gospel, he has been embroiled in controversy with religious authorities who oppose his ministry. At the center of those debates stands Jesus' provocative statement: "I am the light of the world" (8:12). Jesus is not *a* light, one among many; he is *the* light, the one in and through whom God's eternal light is shattering the world's darkness.

Now, as Jesus exits the temple (8:59b), he and his disciples pass a man "blind from birth." Reflecting the assumptions of their place and time—that all illness was the result of sin—the disciples ask the cause of this man's plight: is his own sin or that of his parents responsible (v. 2)? Jesus rejects any absolute connection between sin and illness and reframes the man's predicament as an opportunity for God to bring light and life to one who is blind (vv. 3-5). Once more Jesus declares himself the "light of the world" (v. 5), tying this narrative to the chapter and controversy that precedes it (8:12).

The story of the healing proper begins with Jesus mixing dirt with his own spittle and rubbing the pasty substance into the man's eyes (v. 6); perhaps Jesus did this to inspire hope since a holy man's saliva was considered to have medicinal value. The man is then sent to the Pool of Siloam (meaning "Sent" as the man is *sent*, v. 7), where he washes the paste from his eyes as Jesus commanded. When the man trusts in Jesus ("believes," 3:12) and does what he commands ("follows," 8:12b), his sight is restored: "Then he went and washed and *came back able to see*" (v. 7).

As the story unfolds, it becomes clear that Jesus intends on healing not just this man's physical blindness, but his deeper spiritual blindness as well. Indeed, in this highly symbolic Gospel, the invitation to "come and *see*" is pregnant with meaning. In chapter 1, Jesus invites Andrew and John into the pilgrimage of discipleship with the words, "*Come and see*" (1:39). As they begin to perceive the light of God dawning in Jesus, they tease Nathaniel into moving toward Jesus with the same challenge: "*Come and see*" (1:46). In chapter 4, when the woman at the well bears her witness to Jesus, she exclaims, "*Come and see* a man who told me everything I have ever done!" (4:29). At the tomb of Lazarus—where, short of Easter, Jesus' light will blaze most brightly—Mary and Martha beckon Jesus to their brother's tomb with the words that mean more than they know: "*Come and see*" (11:34). Very shortly, they shall.

But for the man born blind, the faith to see clearly who Jesus is—and who *he* can be because of Jesus—does not come easily or instantaneously. Instead, for him as for believers in every place and time, there is a gradual but deepening comprehension of Jesus' divine glory and grace.

The first scene depicting the physical healing (9:1-7) is followed by a second scene where those who know the once-blind man question him (9:8-12). Some think he is the same person, but some do not. When they ask, "How were your eyes opened?" (v. 10), he can only attribute his newfound sight to "the *man called Jesus*" (v. 11).

The third scene (9:13-17) features the first of two interrogations by the religious authorities. Many of the Pharisees refuse to believe God would heal a man born blind; their theology connecting sin and sickness does not permit such a thing to happen (v. 16). They refuse to "see" the truth of what God is doing in Jesus, while the man born blind simply reports his healing at Jesus' hand (v. 15) and wonders aloud how a certifiable "sinner" could perform such a remarkable act of healing (v. 16). When pressed, the man offers his confession that Jesus is a *prophet* (v. 17).

In the fourth scene, the man's parents are brought in for questioning (9:18-24). They verify their son's identity but refuse to be drawn into the debate lest they be "put out" of the synagogue for expressing faith in Jesus.

Next follows scene five (9:24-34), where the authorities summon the once-blind man yet again and tell him the testimony they want to hear: "Denounce this Jesus as a *sinner*" (v. 24). But this stalwart soul refuses to turn his back on Jesus, making instead the winsome confession, "Once I was blind, now I see!" (v. 25).

The grilling intensifies, as does this man's resistance to being manipulated and manhandled. He becomes testy and assertive, asking those who would twist the truth to make it fit their preconceptions, "Do you also want to become his disciples?" (v. 27).

The authorities are outraged, confessing their faith in Moses but saying of Jesus, "We do not know where this man comes from" (v. 29).

With ever increasing understanding and courage, the man declares Jesus "*a man from God*" (v. 33). The Pharisees respond by dismissing this witness as a "sinner" and throw him out (cf. v. 34).

In the sixth and final scene of the story (9:35-41), Jesus seeks and finds the outcast. For twenty-eight verses, Jesus has been offstage; now suddenly he appears. As microbiologist George Fearnehough once observed, "Jesus said, 'I am the light of the world.' And the most remarkable thing about light is the speed of its coming!"

Now in the healed man's second encounter with Jesus, a growing faith blossoms into a full confession: "'Lord, I believe.' And he worshiped him" (v. 37). Thus, this man's physical healing is complemented by a fuller, spiritual healing as illumination about Jesus' true identity shatters the darkness in his soul. Now this man knows in his heart of hearts that Jesus is indeed "the light of the world" (8:12). Now he sees clearly that Jesus is the *Son of Man* (v. 35), the *Lord* (v. 38), *God's one and only Son* (3:16) in whom true life is found.

By contrast, those who refuse to see the light of God's truth in Jesus bring judgment upon themselves: by choosing to live in the darkness of disbelief, they choose the spiritual death the darkness brings (v. 39; 3:18-19). Such willful blindness is the essence of "sin" (vv. 40-41).

Keep Yonder Light in Your Eye

As every amateur astronomer knows, the deeper the night, the brighter the stars. The brilliance of Jesus' light is directly proportional to the depth of one's darkness. The man born blind represents the deepest darkness of all: pitch black helplessness and despair. Even there, even then, Jesus delivered this man because the man had faith to "see."

In whatever darkness we find ourselves—the darkness of doubt, the darkness of despair, the darkness of fear—Jesus is the God-light shining in the darkness, beckoning us toward himself, that is, toward life abundant and life eternal.

In John Bunyan's epic work, *Pilgrim's Progress*, Evangelist points across a wide field. "Do you see yonder gate?" he asks the Pilgrim.

"No," Pilgrim answers.

"Then," says Evangelist, "do you see yonder shining light?"

"Yes," says the Pilgrim, "I think I do."

"Then keep that light in your eye," says Evangelist. "Keep that in your eye."

That's the essence of being a Christian: no matter how thick or impenetrable the darkness, keep the God-light of Jesus Christ in your eye.

1. What was the darkest *physical* darkness you ever experienced? Describe the relief you felt at the return of light.

2. Describe one of the darkest *spiritual* moments in your life. Who or what became the "light" shining in your darkness?

3. In addition to the focal passages of this lesson (John 1:4-5, 9; 8:12; 9:1-41), consider other passages in this Gospel and John's letters where Jesus appears as the light in the darkness: John 3:19-21; 8:12; 9:4-5; 11:9-10; 12:35-6, 46; 1 John 1:6-7; 2:8-9. What other insights do you find about Jesus as the light and about the darkness that resists him?

4. What does it mean to say Jesus is the "true light" (1:9)? What is a false light? Ponder the difference between the sun's natural light and the artificial light inside a building. Apply the contrast to the difference between Jesus and other "lesser" lights.

5. Compare Jesus' comment on sin and suffering in John 9:3 (and Luke 13:1-5) with his comment on the same subject in John 5:14. Explore the difference between the two stories (and the two leading characters) that evokes such seemingly contradictory statements from Jesus.

6. Compare the blind man's growing faith in Jesus as it appears in vv. 11, 17, 25, 33, 35, 38 with the story of the woman at the well where a similar progression occurs (4:1-42). What does the motif of growing recognition in these two stories suggest about coming to faith in Jesus as the "light of the world"?

7. Many commentators, ancient and modern, see in the blind man's washing in the Pool of Siloam (vv. 6-12) a symbolic reference to baptism. In what ways is Christian baptism a "coming to light and life" in Jesus?

8. What can the man born blind, now healed, teach us about sharing our faith in Jesus and helping others "see the light"? What are this man's most winsome qualities, his most effective moves, and his most memorable statements?

Session 3

Signs

John 2:1-22; 6:1-15, 22-69

It's one of those stories too good *not* to be true.

In the years following World War II, a pastor in Brooklyn faced a pressing problem. Just days before the all-important Christmas Eve service, a terrible storm blew through and a roof leak dislodged a large piece of plaster above and behind the pulpit.

Later, while wondering what to do, the pastor came upon a sidewalk sale. There he bought a beautiful, hand-crocheted tablecloth emblazoned with a large cross that would perfectly cover the church's ruined wall.

Arriving back at the church, the pastor saw an elderly lady sitting in the cold by a bus stop. He invited her to warm herself inside the church while she waited. She sat quietly in a pew as he got a ladder, hoisted the tablecloth, and mounted it on the wall. Then he turned to see the elderly lady staring ashen faced at the tablecloth.

"Pastor," she asked in a trembling voice, "where did you get that tablecloth?"

He told her, and she asked if the initials "E. B. G." were crocheted in the lower right corner. They were.

It turned out that this very lady had sewn the tablecloth years before in her native Austria. When the Nazis came, she was forced to flee, leaving all her worldly possessions behind. Her husband was to follow a week later, but he was captured, sent to prison, and never heard from again.

After hearing this story, the pastor drove the badly shaken woman home to a little apartment on the other side of Staten Island.

At the Christmas Eve service, everyone was captivated by the lovely tablecloth with the embroidered cross, especially one elderly gentleman. After the service, the man asked the pastor where the tablecloth was from. It was identical to one his wife had made in Austria some years before. Then the old man told the story of the Nazis coming, the flight of his wife, and his own imprisonment.

"Might I take you for a short ride?" asked the pastor. "There's someone I want you to meet." He drove the man to a little apartment on the other side of Staten Island. The two men walked up three flights of stairs, the pastor knocked on the door, and then he witnessed a most remarkable and beautiful reunion.

That touching story landed in my e-mail box last Christmas. According to the Snopes website—a site devoted to debunking Internet legends—this story, though difficult to verify, may be true.

To many people of faith, such stories sound like a "God thing." It seems impossible that all those circumstances could line up so perfectly by accident. Certainly, skeptics can and do dismiss such stories, but people with a heart for God believe God's mighty works aren't just something from Bible times; those mighty works continue still today. Indeed, one reason people forward inspirational emails is because such stories touch a tender place inside where we yearn to believe God is still active in our lives in a vital, personal way.

The Sign Language of Faith

John's Gospel has a special word for uncanny events that suggest the living God has drawn near: John calls these events "signs." Indeed, when Jesus turns the water into wine at the wedding in Cana, John whispers from offstage, "This was the first of Jesus' *signs*" (2:11). Such "signs" do more than attract attention to Jesus' mighty works; they reveal the essence of God's "glory" in him (2:11b).

By contrast, when this word, "sign," is used in the first three Gospels, it is almost always used in a negative sense. For example, in Mark 8, some religious leaders come to Jesus demanding a "sign." Jesus sighs and answers, "Why does this generation ask for a *sign*? Truly I tell you, no *sign* will be given to this generation" (Mark 8:12).

In John's Gospel, seven stately "signs" provide decisive clues as to who Jesus is: (1) the changing of the water into wine (2:1-11), (2) the healing of the royal official's son (4:46-54), (3) the healing of the paralytic (5:1-15), (4) the feeding of the five thousand (6:1-15), (5) Jesus walking on the water (6:16-22), (6) the healing of the man born blind (9:1-41), and (7) the raising of Lazarus

(11:1-44). Clearly, Jesus did many more signs than these seven, as John readily admits (20:30). But these seven were chosen "so you may come to believe that Jesus is the Messiah, the Son of God" (20:31). In the Bible, the number seven indicates perfection or completion. John believes *seven* signs are enough to give one full or "perfect" knowledge of who Jesus is.

Further, in John's Gospel, each sign functions at two levels: (1) a wonder-evoking level that points to Jesus' command over illness, disability, nature, and even death and (2) a meaning-rich level where Jesus' "glory" or divine essence is revealed (2:11). As in the first three Gospels, Jesus refuses to "entrust himself" to a faith based on signs, knowing such a faith is superficial and self-serving (2:23-25; Matt 16:4; Luke 11:29-30; see also John 2:18-19; 6:30). However, John's Gospel proclaims Jesus' signs have the power to point beyond themselves to the One whose glory they reveal (9:16; 10:38). Indeed, when the signs point a spiritual seeker toward Jesus as Son of God and Savior (4:42), they fulfill their divinely appointed purpose (2:11; 20:30-31).

Thus, there is an interesting tension in John's Gospel. On the one hand, there is an appreciation for what might be called the "sign language" of faith, those moments of wonder and surprise when one senses God is near. On the other hand, there is a deep suspicion of any faith that can be *reduced* to signs. Fascination with *signs* is not the mark of an authentic Christian faith; fascination with *Jesus* is the mark of an authentic Christian faith.

The Wedding at Cana (2:1-11)

In the story of the wedding at Cana, we encounter the first of John's seven signs (2:1-11). In this story, the sign of Jesus turning water into wine serves its holy purpose: it awakens faith in Jesus as the One in whom the living God is decisively present (v. 11).

The story begins with a crisis when the wine runs out at a wedding. Jesus' mother knows this is a problem he can solve. She slips over to him and whispers, "They have no wine" (v. 3).

Jesus replies in a most abrupt manner, calling her only "Woman" (v. 4). In John's Gospel, Mary, the mother of Jesus, is never called by name. In fact, the only other time Jesus addresses his mother in this Gospel, he uses the same brusque term, "Woman" (19:26). The thrust of Jesus' remark seems to be that he will not be pressured into revealing his glory prematurely. Nonetheless, his mother's confidence in him is unshaken. She instructs the servants, "Do whatever he tells you" (v. 5).

Despite his reservations, Jesus proceeds to act. Noting six stone water jars used for the ceremonial washing of guests' hands and feet (v. 6), Jesus instructs the servants to top off the jars with fresh water. They are then to draw off some of the liquid and take it to the chief steward.

When the chief steward tastes the "water that had become wine," he is delighted to discover the bridegroom has reserved the best wine for last (v. 10)! Only the servants and the disciples realize what really happened since Jesus acted quietly and without fanfare (v. 9b).

Jesus' disciples respond with a deepening faith in him. In addition to their astonishment at the water becoming wine (the wonder level of the sign), they also see God's "glory" in Jesus (the significance level of the sign). As John is careful to note, "Jesus did this, the first of his *signs,* in Cana of Galilee, and revealed his *glory;* and his disciples *believed* in him" (v. 11).

The first of Jesus' "signs" at the wedding in Cana foreshadows all the ways Jesus will transform conventional religion. In his presence, the flat, tepid water of religion-as-usual will become the sparkling, delicious wine of a vital, Spirit-filled faith (1:33; 3:5-8; Acts 2:4, 13). The new life Jesus brings will be given "without measure" (3:34), expressing "grace upon grace" (1:16). One hundred twenty gallons is a lot of wine (v. 6)!

The Cleansing of the Temple (2:13-22)

The positive use of a "sign" as revealing Jesus' glory in John 2:1-12 contrasts sharply with the negative use of the term in the next passage, the story of Jesus' cleansing of the temple (2:13-22). After Jesus throws out those turning his "Father's house into a marketplace" (v. 16), the religious authorities come storming up and demand, "What *sign* can you show us for doing this?" (v. 18). They want indisputable proof that Jesus is a Messianic figure with the right to challenge and reform the worship of the temple, a not altogether unreasonable demand.

Jesus responds cryptically, "Destroy this temple, and in three days I will raise it up" (v. 19). While the meaning of this statement is not initially apparent, the disciples later realize in light of Easter that Jesus was talking about the "temple of his body" (v. 21). Jesus *himself* is the new temple where God and humanity will meet

(4:20-24; 14:6; Hebrews 10:19-23). The life, death, and resurrection of Jesus are the decisive "sign" of who Jesus is and what God is accomplishing in and through him (v. 22).

John's story of the cleansing of the temple is followed by a brief epilogue that notes, "Many believed in his name because they saw the *signs* that he was doing" (v. 23b). While John uses the phrase, "believed in [Jesus'] name," here as in 1:12, clearly there is something inadequate or preliminary about this faith, for Jesus will not "entrust himself" to those who thus believe (v. 24). Perhaps the meaning is that many who saw Jesus' signs failed to see *past* or *through* the sign to the glory of God that was decisively present in God's Son-in-the-flesh (1:14, 18). The signs were not meant to point to themselves, but to *him.*

The Bread of Life (6:1-15, 22-69)

In the sixth chapter of John's Gospel, the tension between a faith based in *signs* and a faith based in *Jesus* comes to a head. Jesus takes a little boy's lunch, multiplies the bread and fish, and feeds five thousand people (6:1-14). This is yet another sign of Jesus' compassion and God's power to make a difference in the face of human need (6:2, 14).

The next morning, the crowds chase Jesus to the other side of the Sea of Galilee (6:22-24). They arrive, eager for Jesus to feed them breakfast, but Jesus refuses to dole out a second helping. Instead, he confronts the crowd, saying, "Very truly, I tell you, you are looking for me, not because you saw signs, but because you ate your fill of the loaves" (v. 25). "Do not work for the food that perishes," Jesus pleads, "but for the food that [gives] eternal life" (v. 26).

In Paddy Chayefsky's play, *Gideon*, God says, "I meant for you to love me but you were only curious." One senses Jesus coming to the same conclusion as the tense encounter between himself and the crowd unfolds. Jesus tells the people that the essence of a true and living faith is to "believe in him whom [God] has sent" (v. 29), and they respond, "What *sign* are you going to give us then, so that we may *see* it and *believe* you?" (v. 30). Refusing to see or believe that Jesus himself is the all-important sign from God, they insist on a stupendous event that will compel their faith.

Finally, Jesus clearly tells them (and us!), "*I* am the bread of life. Whoever comes to me will never be hungry, and whoever believes in me will never be thirsty" (v. 35; 4:13-15). This is the first of the seven great "I Am" sayings found in John's Gospel (a matter treated more fully in session 6 of this book). The point of the "I am" sayings is to point beyond signs with a lowercase "s" (feeding the multitude) to the "Sign"—capital "S"—of who Jesus is: the Bread of Life.

The crowds are not pleased by the prospect of no more free lunches, despite the fact that Jesus himself is God's gift of sustaining grace for all of time and eternity (vv. 40, 47-48, 51). Their disappointment turns to malice (vv. 41-42), and the conflict intensifies (vv. 52, 60) until, finally, a crowd of Jesus' would-be followers desert him in droves (v. 66).

Only Jesus' inner circle, the Twelve Disciples, remains (v. 67). Weary and disappointed, Jesus turns to the Twelve and asks plaintively, "Do you also wish to go away?" (v. 67).

Simon Peter answers for them and for all true disciples in every place and time: "Lord, to whom can we go? *You* have the words of eternal life!" (v. 68).

Sooner or later, that moment of decision comes for us all: the moment when the miracles run out and the special signs we long for disappear. We are left to decide if we will love Jesus for who he is or only because of what we hope he will do for us.

Professor, author, and evangelist Tony Campolo tells about praying for the healing of a man, gravely ill with cancer, who subsequently died. Several days later, the man's wife called. Naturally, Campolo dreaded having to talk about the "failure" of his prayer for healing.

But the woman on the phone wasn't accusing, only grateful. She said that before Campolo prayed for her husband, her husband was bitter and angry, estranged from God and everyone else.

"But then you laid hands on him that Sunday," said the caller, "and prayed with him. As we walked out of the church, I could tell something was different. I could feel it. The last few days we spent together were the best in our marriage. We talked and laughed and reminisced. We even sang hymns together. It was a blessed time."

The woman on the other end of the line paused, gathered herself, and said, "Tony, my husband wasn't *cured,* but he was *healed.*"

The miracles we hope for and pray for are not the be-all and end-all of an authentic Christian faith. Instead, the heart of our faith is Jesus Christ and the deeper healing he brings, namely, the assurance of God's love, presence, and peace, no matter what. Jesus is the Sign above and beyond every other, the one who brings the living God near. The greatest gift Jesus can ever give is the gift of *himself*. "It is *I*! Do not be afraid" (6:20).

As we will see again and again in John's Gospel, while signs can point us to Jesus, there is a world of difference between faith in *signs* and faith in *him*.

1. In what ways does Jesus turn the water of a life without him into the wine of a rich, full life where he is Lord and master? What qualities of "good wine" (v. 10) speak to your experience of Jesus?

____

____

____

____

____

2. Can you relate the story of a sign that deepened your faith? What about the experience drew you closer to God?

____

____

____

____

____

3. Talk about the difference between a faith open to signs and a faith focused on them. Why does Jesus show such suspicion about a faith that can be reduced to signs? (See also Matthew 12:38-40; Mark 8:11-12; and Luke 11:16, 29-30.)

4. Notice how Jesus reinterprets the miracle of the manna as pointing to himself (6:31-35). How might this be a model for interpreting or *re*interpreting other Bible stories about miracles?

5. Can you tell about a time when the sign you hoped and prayed for never came? How did God or God's people guide and sustain you nonetheless?

6. Briefly review the seven signs in John's Gospel, as listed on page 29. List the key truth about Jesus to which each sign points.

7. Complete the following confession in twenty-five words or less: "To me, Jesus is the Sign above every other sign *that* . . . ."

The Seven Signs of John's Gospel	
1	The Changing of the Water into Wine, 2:1-11
2	The Healing of the Royal Official's Son, 4:46-54
3	The Healing of the Paralytic, 5:1-15
4	The Feeding of the Five Thousand, 6:1-15
5	Jesus Walking on Water, 6:16-22
6	The Healing of the Man Born Blind, 9:1-41
7	The Raising of Lazarus, 11:1-44

Session 4

Born Again

John 3:1-18

Last fall, a hospital in my community sponsored a men's health clinic. Along with offering free medical tests, the clinic gave medical providers an opportunity to promote their services. One exhibitor promoted a newly opened sleep clinic.

As I chatted with Ron, the gentleman manning the booth, I asked about an annoying twitching of my legs that sometimes disturbed my (and my wife's!) sleep. I wondered if it might be restless leg syndrome. Ron said my description sounded more like a symptom of sleep apnea. Having been diagnosed and treated for this condition himself, Ron was evangelistic in his zeal for getting other sufferers the help they needed. He said that upon waking the first morning after wearing a CPAP (continuous positive airway pressure) mask to ensure his oxygen flow, he felt alert and clear-headed, startled by how bright and beautiful the world appeared.

Ron persuaded me to have a sleep test to see if I had sleep apnea. To my surprise, it turned out I did. Sure enough, just as Ron promised, the morning after wearing my CPAP mask the first time, I awoke to a whole new world. My head was clear of the usual grogginess, my vision was sharper, colors were crisper, the sky was brighter, and I was full of vigor. Never before had I slept so well or greeted the day with such energy, optimism, and joy.

In the third chapter of John's Gospel, we meet a man suffering from sleep apnea of the soul. This man's spirit starves for the renewing breath of the Spirit of God. As a result, he cannot see clearly or act with wisdom, vitality, or decisiveness. His name is Nicodemus.

Jesus' Encounter with Nicodemus (3:1-10)

Nicodemus comes to Jesus "by night" (v. 2). Perhaps he did this in part to hide his interest in a controversial religious teacher, but in this highly symbolic Gospel, "night" also symbolizes the spiritual darkness of unbelief (3:19; 11:10; 13:30). Indeed, we can read this passage as a dramatic commentary on John 1:5: "The darkness cannot *understand* the light" (NIV). While Nicodemus is a respected religious leader, he cannot clearly see or discern God's truth (vv. 3, 10).

Like many would-be believers then and now, Nicodemus is attracted by the "signs" he sees Jesus doing (v. 2), but as we have seen, there is a big difference between faith in *signs* and faith in *Jesus.* Nicodemus has the first but not yet the second. It remains to be seen whether the light of God in Jesus Christ will pierce Nicodemus's spiritual blindness.

Jesus waves aside Nicodemus's intended compliment (v. 2) and tells him plainly, "Very truly, I tell you, no one can see the kingdom of God without being born from above" (v. 3). God's kingdom cannot be entered through moral or intellectual effort, but only through a profound spiritual transformation that Jesus likens to a new birth. "Seeing" God's kingdom dawning in Jesus requires that one be born "from above" (NRSV) or born "again" (vv. 3 and 7, KJV and NIV).

The Greek word underlying the English translation, "from above" or "again," can carry either meaning, depending on the context. In John 3:3 and 3:7, probably both meanings are intended. "From *above*" emphasizes the *origin* of the new life Jesus gives; this life is given by the One descending from the heavenly realm to reveal the truth about God (v. 13; 1:1-18). "Born *again*" emphasizes the *quality* of the new life Jesus gives: one's life *after* trusting in Jesus brings such a radical new beginning that it's like being born again!

Nicodemus responds with plodding literalism, completely missing Jesus' point (v. 4). Jesus tries again, elaborating his meaning (v. 5). With the solemn declaration, "Very truly"—used three times in this passage (vv. 3, 5, 11)—Jesus challenges Nicodemus to understand the nature of spiritual rebirth. No one can "see" (v. 3) or "enter" (v. 5) the kingdom of God without being born of "water and Spirit." Jesus probably intends to contrast the birth waters of one's first, physical birth—"What is born of the flesh is flesh" (v. 6a)—

with the desperately needed second birth by the Spirit: "And what is born of the Spirit is spirit" (v. 6b).

Seeing Nicodemus still does not grasp his meaning, Jesus implores him, "Do not be astonished that I said to you, 'You must be born from above [or "again"]'" (v. 7). Jesus then employs the figure of the wind to suggest the presence and power of God's Spirit. In both Hebrew and Greek, the original languages of the Bible, the word translated "Spirit" can also be translated "Wind." The Spirit of God, like the wind, is mysterious and mighty, moving when and as it will.

Nicodemus still doesn't "get it" (vv. 9-10), but we owe one of the richest chapters in the Bible to his inability to understand. Jesus' repeated attempts to pierce Nicodemus's and our blindness with the light of God's truth yields a rich constellation of images to ponder: being "born again," the Spirit and the wind, ascending to and descending from heaven (v. 13), a serpent in the wilderness (v. 14), God's only Son (v. 15), eternal life (v. 16), and more.

By v. 11, Jesus appears to give up on Nicodemus, at least for now, as Nicodemus disappears from the story and is not mentioned again. Still, Jesus presses on because he is after bigger game than just Nicodemus. Jesus is after the entire world. Jesus is after *you.*

The New Birth

A little boy of four couldn't wait for his new sister to come home from the hospital. He wanted to be near her, to talk with her, to have time alone with her. His parents were reluctant to leave their newborn alone with a four-year-old, but he was so insistent that they finally relented.

One night, the parents watched discreetly from the baby's bedroom door as the boy tiptoed to his sister's crib. Leaning near, he whispered, "Tell me about God. I'm starting to forget."

The new birth, the new life Jesus comes to bring does not begin with our respectable, grown-up, Nicodemus self. The new birth, the new life Jesus brings begins with our vulnerable, trusting, childlike self asking Jesus to breathe *his* life, *his* love, *his* strength into us. Only then can we discover our lost identity and true destiny as sons and daughters of God (1:12; Mark 10:15).

I still remember, as a boy of nine, waking up the morning after I became a Christian and feeling a warmth and strength inside that wasn't there before. I didn't understand much about the experience then, and there's much about it that I don't understand now. But after asking Jesus to be my Lord and Savior, I lived with a riveting awareness that has never left me: Jesus lives within me, and I belong to him now and forever.

Such a new birth experience is central to John's understanding of what it means to be a believer. This guiding metaphor is found both in the Gospel (ch. 3) and in the letters bearing his name (1 John 2:29; 3:9; 5:1, 18). To be "born again" or "born from above" means the Spirit of God, God's own life and presence, comes to indwell the believer (Titus 3:5-6; 1 Pet 1:3, 23).

One of the ways the New Testament describes this experience is to be "baptized," literally, "immersed" in the Holy Spirit (John 1:33; Acts 2:38). To be "baptized in the Holy Spirit" is not the experience of the select few; it is the birthright of *every* believer (Rom 8:9). This baptism, this new birth made possible through faith in Jesus Christ, is also the fulfillment of the earnest old covenant hope that someday God's Spirit would indwell *all* God's children (Ezek 36:26-27; Jer 31:31-34; Acts 2:17-18).

Indeed, restoring the divine breath or Spirit to a world suffocating for want of spiritual life is part of God's plan for recreating the world (1:1, 10-12). Following his resurrection, Jesus appears to his disciples in a locked room where they are hiding (20:19-23). He bids them his peace, *breathes* on them, and says, "Receive the Holy Spirit" (v. 22). This divine breath that gives life recalls God's creation of Adam: "Then the LORD God formed man from the dust of the ground, and *breathed* into his nostrils the *breath of life*; and the man became a living being" (Gen 2:7). Even so, on the far side of Jesus' death and resurrection, he is ready to recreate the world of those who trust in him (2 Cor 5:17). He does this in large measure by the power of his indwelling Spirit, the Spirit of life (6:63; 7:37-39).

I don't remember my first breath as the baby boy of Bob and Belva Setzer. I don't remember my first breath as a child of God. But as surely as my physical life began when I first sucked in the air of a new world, so the Christian life is possible only as the Holy Spirit breathes life into my feeble efforts to follow Jesus. It is because of the Spirit's presence within, the divine breath of eternal life, that one is able to "see" who Jesus is and who one is called to be because of him.

In the story of the woman at the well (John 4) is an especially vivid image of the Holy Spirit's presence in the life of the believer: "living water" (4:10). "Living water" is a bubbling spring water as opposed to the still water of a well or pond. Instead of the ordinary water of the well (or the six water jars at the wedding in Cana, 2:6), Jesus offers water to quench one's spiritual thirst, becoming in those who believe "a spring of water gushing up to eternal life" (4:13-14). In John 7:37-39, the reader is told plainly that the "living water" refers to the gift of the Holy Spirit, the divine center of the new life Jesus gives.

Best of all, the Holy Spirit is not an impersonal power like wind or breath or water, but a personal Presence who brings Jesus near (John 14:18-19, 25-27). We will explore John's special word for the nature and work of the Holy Spirit, the *Paraclete*, in session 9 of this book.

Recently, a member of our church told me about his own deepening experience of God's Spirit and Presence: "It's not like I *have* to go to church; I am *drawn* to this church. I feel like for the first time, I'm in the main current of the river, being borne along by the waters, my muscles working only to keep me in position to ride the waves. No longer am I stuck in an eddy, side current, or behind a rock."

The new life Jesus gives transforms the "have tos" of our Nicodemus self into the "want tos" of the Spirit-filled self (Eph 5:18). It's the difference in a life lived through our own ceaseless efforts and a life lived in the awareness of God's indwelling presence, power, and peace.

Believe and Receive Eternal Life (3:11-18)

The new birth and new life made possible through the indwelling presence of the Holy Spirit begins by *believing* in Jesus (vv. 15-16). Such belief is far more than mere intellectual assent to a proposition; it is entrusting oneself to a person. In John's Gospel, to "believe" in Jesus means to love and trust Jesus and to reorient one's life around him.

Two essential elements of such belief in Jesus are spelled out in John 3:13-16. First, Jesus is the *Savior* (4:42), the "Lamb of God" who comes to "take away the sin of the world" (1:29). In his death, Jesus will be "lifted up" on the cross as Moses lifted the serpent in the wilderness (vv. 13-14; Num 21:1-9; John 12:32-33). This shattering revelation of God's sacrificial love in the death of God's Son will bring forgiveness, healing, and new life to those who believe (vv. 15-16).

Second, Jesus is the *Lord* (6:68; 9:38; 11:27; 20:28), the One in whom God is present in a decisive and personal way. John coined a special word to describe Jesus' unique relationship to God. This word (the Greek word *monogenes*) is a compound of the two words, "mono," literally meaning "single" or "only," and "genes," the basis of our English word "genus," meaning "class" or "kind"—God's "one-of-a-kind" Son (1:14, 18; 3:16, 18). The traditional King James rendering of the word, "Only begotten" Son, makes the point that Jesus alone was from God and of God from the beginning (1:1-3). While the conviction that Jesus is God's unique Son is found throughout the New Testament (see, for example, Matt 11:27; 1 Cor 8:6; Col 1:15-16; Eph 1:3-6; Heb 1:1-5), the word *monogenes* is John's alone (found in 1:14, 18; 3:16, 18; 1 John 4:9).

Thus, those who "believe" in Jesus as "Savior" and "Lord" receive the gift of "eternal life" (3:15-16), meaning both "forever" life and life lived *now* in the presence and peace of God's indwelling Spirit (3:36). Through such a life-changing relationship with Jesus, one escapes the darkness of condemnation (v. 18) and judgment (v. 19) to live abundantly now (10:10) *and* forever (11:25-26).

Some Bible translators in Papua, New Guinea, worked to render the phrase "born again" from John 3:3, 5. Finally, a native speaker suggested an approach: "Sometimes a person goes wrong and will not listen to anybody. We all get together in the village and place that person in the midst of us. The elders talk to him for a long time. 'You have gone wrong!' they say. 'All your thoughts, intentions, and values are wrong. Now you have to become a baby again and start to relearn everything right.'"

Hence, in that version of the New Testament, John 3:3 reads, "No one can see the kingdom of God unless he becomes like a baby again and relearns everything from God's word."

Through faith in Jesus Christ and the indwelling presence of the Holy Spirit, the gift of new life is given. No matter how difficult or deplorable one's past, Jesus has the power to give a new birth, a new beginning. What he was by nature, we can become by a spiritual rebirth: sons and daughters of God: "He came to what was his own, and his own people did not accept him. But to all who received him, who believed in his name, he gave power to become children of God, who were born, not of blood or of the will of the flesh or of the will of man, but of God" (1:11-12).

It's a lot to be thankful for. Every day when I wake up and feel the tremor of Jesus' divine life nesting within my own mortal selfhood, I am thankful beyond words.

1. Why did Nicodemus have such a hard time understanding Jesus? What about Jesus do you have a hard time understanding?

____

____

____

____

____

2. Do you prefer the translation "born again" or "born from above"? Why? Compare Bible translations online or in print to see how this phrase is rendered.

____

____

____

____

____

3. Have you experienced or witnessed the birth of a child? How does that recollection shape your image of the "new birth"?

____

____

____

____

____

4. Baptists are among the Christian groups that emphasize the importance of being "born again." Why is that experience so crucial to a vital Christian faith?

5. How is the wind a particularly apt metaphor of the movements of God's Spirit? Can you describe an experience where the wind deeply moved or renewed you? Has God's Spirit ever done the same?

6. What do you find most hopeful or reassuring in Jesus' image of the Holy Spirit as a wellspring within the believer (4:13-14; 7:37-39)?

7. John 3:16 has been called "the gospel in a nutshell." Do you agree with this characterization? How many key words or themes of the gospel can you identify in this verse?

8. Read more about Nicodemus in John 7:50-51 and 19:39. Do you believe Nicodemus came to a true and genuine faith in Jesus? Read the Wikipedia article about him online (http://en.wikipedia.org/wiki/Nicodemus) or consult another source and see how Christian tradition answers that question.

Session 5

B[illegible]

John 3:17-21; 4:1-42;

Shortly after his marriage, the nineteenth-century Irish poet Thomas Moore was called away on business. Upon his return, the family doctor greeted him. "Your wife is upstairs," said the physician, "but she has asked that you not come up." It was then that Thomas Moore learned the terrible truth: his once beautiful wife had contracted small pox. The disease left her flawless skin pocked and marred. After taking one look at herself in the mirror, she commanded that the shutters be drawn and that her husband never see her again.

Ignoring her wishes, Moore ran upstairs and threw open the door of his wife's room. It was pitch black inside. Groping along the wall, Moore felt for the gas jets. A startled cry came from a black corner of the room: "No! Don't light the lamps, Thomas!" Moore hesitated, swayed by the pleading voice. "Go!" she begged. "Please *go*! This is the greatest gift you can give."

Moore left and went to his study. There he stayed up most of the night, prayerfully writing not just a poem, but a song.

The next morning as soon as the sun rose, he returned to his wife's room. He felt his way to a chair and sat down. "Are you awake?" he asked.

"I am," came a voice from the far side of the room. "But you must not ask to see me. You must not press me, Thomas."

"I will sing to you then," he answered. And at that, Thomas Moore began to sing of his abiding love.

As he sang, there was stirring in the dark corner where his wife waited in her loneliness. Then, as Moore's voice trailed off on the last note of his song, he heard his bride rise. She crossed the room

.. the window, reached up, and slowly drew open the shutters. In the morning light, he saw her pocked face and loved her still.

When someone is hiding in the dark, light creates a crisis. It creates the crisis of exposing one who wants to stay hidden. It creates the crisis of revealing ugly, unseemly truths. It creates the crisis of stinging and blinding the dark-adjusted eyes of those who behold the light.

Those who can bear the light may well find hope and healing. But those who renounce the light to hide in the dark choose hopelessness and despair. *That*, says John's Gospel, is the crisis Jesus brings: "This is the *Crisis*, that the light has come into the world, and people loved darkness rather than light because their deeds were evil" (3:19).

The Crisis Jesus Brings (3:17-21)

The Greek word translated "judgment" in John 3:19 is *krisis*, the basis of the English word "crisis." It was not God's intention to *condemn*, but to *save* the world by the sending of God's Son (v. 17). Nonetheless, Jesus' coming creates an inevitable crisis. The searing light of God's truth in him reveals the depths of the world's darkness and exposes those who wish to keep their evil deeds hidden (v. 19). Such persons "hate" and resist the light, doing their best to destroy it (8:37, 43-47; 11:49-53) or, lacking that, to flee its enfolding rays (18:15-27).

Sadly, those who reject the light of God in Jesus choose a fate of spiritual darkness and death. In the spiritual realm, as in the biological realm, life flourishes where there is light (1:4). A houseplant consigned to a shadowy corner, out of the reach of the sun or other light, soon "perishes" (3:16). According to John's Gospel, people do too.

For those who stubbornly insist on the darkness of unbelief in God's Son, "condemnation" results. This is not a condemnation God decrees so much as a condemnation one brings upon oneself (v. 18). Nor is judgment confined to the distant future when God will judge the world (Rev 20:11-15). Judgment occurs now as one either embraces the light of God in Jesus Christ or seeks the cover of darkness: "Whoever believes in the Son *has* eternal life; whoever disobeys the Son will not see life, but must endure God's wrath" (3:36), a self-imposed exile from God's presence and peace (Rom 1:18-31).

Thankfully, those who welcome and embrace the light of God's love and truth in Jesus receive life abundant (10:10) and life eternal (3:16). Indeed, John's Gospel was written in the confidence that through faith in Jesus, true life is found: "[These] things are written so that you may come to believe that Jesus is the Messiah, the Son of God, and that through believing you may have *life* in his name" (20:31).

It is said that the Chinese character for "crisis" means "dangerous opportunity." Nowhere is this more true than in one's response to the light of God in Jesus Christ, which shatters the world's spiritual darkness.

Belief: The Woman at the Well (4:1-42)

"Believing" in Jesus—welcoming and living in his light—is given dramatic expression in the story of the woman at the well (John 4). By contrast, what it means to resist Jesus' light and perish in the darkness of unbelief is powerfully illustrated in the story of the paralytic by Beth-Zatha's Pool (John 5). Let us consider each story in turn.

The story of the woman at the well begins as Jesus and his disciples are returning home from the Passover celebration in Jerusalem (2:13, 23; 4:1-3). The text says Jesus "had to go through Samaria" (v. 4b), an area orthodox Jews avoided due to centuries of ethnic tension and hostility. Perhaps Jesus was in a hurry to return to Galilee (4:1-3), and traveling north from Jerusalem through Samaria was the most direct route home. However, one soon suspects something or *Someone* else is dictating Jesus' travel plans.

While his disciples go into the nearby village to buy food (vv. 6, 8), Jesus rests by Jacob's well. In the heat of the day, a lone Samaritan woman comes to draw water (vv. 6b-7). Normally, the women of the village gathered water early in the morning or late in the evening, when it was cool. This woman's coming alone at noon suggests she is shunned.

This woman has every reason to expect she can and will keep Jesus at a distance. Most important, he is a Jew and she a Samaritan (v. 9), normally bitter rivals. Imagine a Jew (like Jesus!) wandering onto the West Bank today (roughly the biblical Samaria) to have a casual chat with a Palestinian. It wasn't done. Further, it was not socially acceptable for a revered religious teacher to converse with a woman in public (v. 27).

After rebuffing Jesus' request for a drink of water (v. 9), the woman's interest is piqued by Jesus' offer of "living water" (v. 10). Taking him literally, she wonders how he will dip such water since he has no bucket. She certainly doesn't plan to do it *for* him (v. 12)! The woman then suggests that compared to the biblical Jacob, Jesus is a nobody (v. 12). Jesus deflects her implied insult and offers "living water," explaining that such water allows one never to thirst again since it becomes "a spring of water gushing up to eternal life" (v. 14; 7:38-39). Intrigued, the woman asks for this "living water" (v. 15).

One might expect the exchange to end here, but the story takes a surprising turn when Jesus tells the woman to go get her husband and come back (v. 16). The woman answers with a half-truth—"I have no husband"—for which Jesus commends her. "You are right in saying, 'I have no husband,'" he says to her, "for you have had *five* husbands, and the one you have now is not your husband. What you have said is true!" (vv. 17-18).

In facing the truth about her serial relationships with men and her own ruinous life, the woman accepts the painful exposure the light of God in Jesus brings. Her trust in Jesus grows: "Sir, I see you are a prophet" (v. 19).

Once more, the woman attempts an evasive maneuver, trying to deflect Jesus' knowing gaze by drawing him into another religious controversy (v. 20). Refusing to take the bait, Jesus declares that the place of worship no longer matters. What "the Father" truly seeks are those who worship "in spirit and *truth*" (vv. 23-24). In coming to terms with the truth about herself—her spiritual destitution and need—and the truth of God's all-knowing but faithful, forgiving love in Jesus, this woman is drawing near to the truth that will set her free (8:32).

The woman tries one more artful dodge of the gospel truth closing in on her, deferring such matters to the Messiah (v. 25). Jesus tells her plainly, "I am he" (v. 26). The woman hastily departs, leaving her water jar behind, asking those in the village, "He cannot be the Messiah, can he?" (v. 29). She further confesses, not once but twice, "He told me everything I have ever done" (vv. 29, 39), yet despite Jesus' knowledge of her tortured past, he still accepts, loves, and forgives her (see also John 8:11). She is being coaxed out of the darkness of self-condemnation (3:18) to live and thrive in Jesus' light.

The story begins with the woman at the well trying to keep Jesus at a distance. But slowly, almost imperceptibly, she comes to trust Jesus and find a new beginning in his light. Her attitude toward Jesus moves from defensive dismissal (v. 9) to tentative trust (vv. 19, 25-26, 29) to full-blown faith (v. 39) in him who is the "Savior of the world" (v. 42). The witness of this female evangelist (despite the reservations of the male disciples, v. 27) leads many others to "believe" and find new life in Jesus' light (v. 39).

Unbelief: The Paralytic by Beth-Zatha's Pool (5:1-18)

Having told a success story about the dawning of faith in Jesus, John's Gospel soon relates a different tale in which the night of unbelief falls: the story of the paralytic by Beth-Zatha's pool (5:1-18).

The story unfolds as sufferers gather in hopes of healing. According to local legend, whenever an angel stirs the water, the first sufferer to enter the pool is healed (v. 7). When Jesus strolls into this wasteland of wrecked, twisted humanity, his eyes fall upon a sufferer more listless and defeated than most. Just by observing the man's demeanor, Jesus can see the man has been lying there "a *long* time" (v. 6), thirty-eight years, in fact. Jesus asks what seems like a foolish question: "Do you *want* to be healed?" (v. 6).

Instinctively, we answer for the sufferer, "Of *course* he wants to be healed!" But instead of giving voice to such a longing, the paralytic responds with the same tired litany of excuses and blame he has recited for years: "Sir, I have no one to put me into the pool when the water is stirred. And whenever I am making my way down, someone always steps in front of me" (v. 7). Apparently, it never occurs to this man to wonder why, in thirty-eight years of trying, he can't summon a single soul to help him!

Could it be that his own negative, caustic spirit leads others to give him wide berth? Or maybe while some part of him wants healing, another part does not? Maybe he's lived as a victim for so long that the freedom and responsibility that go with being a fully functioning adult terrify him. Jesus' question, "Do you want to be healed?" is not as foolish as it might seem.

Because the paralytic by Beth-Zatha's pool can't even summon a qualified "yes" to Jesus' question, Jesus acts in an uncharacteristic way. Usually, he demanded some show of faith before making a sufferer well, but seeing no flicker of faith or hope in the man, Jesus supplies it: "*Stand up, take your mat, and walk*" (v. 8). Immediately, the man is restored to health and begins to walk (v. 9).

Yet while this man experiences a *physical* healing, he does not experience the deeper healing Jesus comes to give. When some law-and-order Pharisees accost the man for carrying his mat on the Sabbath—a technical violation of their rules—he immediately blames Jesus: "The man who made me well told me to do it!" (v. 11). When asked to identify his benefactor, the man doesn't even know Jesus' name. Clearly, he has no interest in Jesus, much less *faith* in Jesus either before or after his healing. Though this man can now *walk,* he remains as crippled *spiritually* as he was before.

In a last effort to reach and transform this man, Jesus seeks him again and offers the solemn warning, "See, you have been made well! Do not sin anymore, so that nothing worse happens to you!" (v. 14). In this instance—as is typical of John's Gospel—"sin" is the sin of unbelief (3:18; 16:8-9). But instead of heeding Jesus' words, the man promptly rats him out to the authorities.

Thus, the story ends in theological fisticuffs (v. 16ff.) between Jesus and his accusers, while the man who started the ruckus slinks toward the shadows and disappears from view. He is Exhibit A in John's Gospel of what it means to reject Jesus and flee his healing light. It's not a pretty picture.

Believing in Jesus

John's Gospel describes faith in a variety of ways. In this instance, as in many others, John twirls a truth like a diamond, letting the light shine through its various facets. Thus, a dawning faith in Jesus can be described as "coming to" (3:20) or "seeing" the light (11:9), "knowing the truth" (8:32; 17:8), "receiving" Jesus (1:12; 17:8), "abiding" in Jesus (15:4-7), and more. But more than any other word, the one in John's Gospel that signifies a trusting, transforming faith in Jesus is the word "believe."

Those who "believe" in Jesus accept his "judgment," the revelation his light brings of their need for forgiveness. But in and through this crisis comes the gift of a most remarkable grace, namely, the new life Jesus gives those who welcome his light, receive his light, and follow his light.

A young man was squandering his life in reckless living. One night, he staggered home drunk in the wee hours of the morning. Hearing him stumble up the stairs, his mother went to his room.

Presently, the father got up and found his wife. She was softly stroking the matted hair of their son, who lay passed out on the bed. "What are you doing?" asked the father.

Her face etched with pain, the mother answered, "I'm loving him. Because he won't let me love him when he's awake."

God's love is steadfast and true whether or not one welcomes and revels in that love. But the full and abundant life Jesus promised is only available to those who awaken to the grace and glory of God in him. This awakening from the darkness of unbelief to the light of a new day is the joy of following Jesus.

The woman by the well found this joy. The paralytic by Beth-Zatha's pool did not.

Which story is most like yours?

1. Describe what it is like to be awakened from a deep sleep by a bright light. What is that experience like?

____

____

____

____

____

2. Can you relate an experience when you were "in the dark," metaphorically speaking, and then "saw the light"? What was good and bad about the experience?

____

____

____

____

____

3. Consider the story of Peter's denial as a case study of how one loses one's way in the darkness of fear and disbelief (18:15-27). Note that this story unfolds at night (18:3, 18).

4. John's Gospel is built around stark contrasts:

Light	Dark
Eternal Life	Perish
Not Condemned	Condemned
Belief	Unbelief
Come to the light	Resist the light

Does this represent simplistic, either/or thinking, or are these poles of a spectrum along which we move? Is faith more like turning on a light or the coming of the dawn?

5. Do you agree that judgment is more a fate we bring upon ourselves or a verdict God decrees?

6. Contrast the story of the paralytic by Beth-zatha's pool (5:1-18) with the story of the man born blind (9:1-41). What qualities about the paralytic reveal the darkness of his disbelief? What qualities about the man born blind show him coming to the Light of Jesus?

7. Can you give examples of a belief that requires risk and commitment versus mere intellectual assent? What does it take to "believe" in Jesus in a way that changes one's life?

8. Which is your preferred way of talking about your faith? "Believing in Jesus" or "following Jesus"? Why?

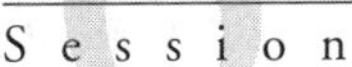

Session

Truth

John 8:12-59; 7:53–8:11

There is probably no saying of Jesus more commonly cited in the hallowed halls of higher learning than John 8:32: "Ye shall know the truth, and the truth shall make you free" (KJV). Indeed, it is not uncommon to see those word emblazoned on university buildings. However, the assumed meaning of the words in such settings—that the unabashed pursuit of intellectual truth will set one free—is *not* what Jesus is talking about in John 8:32.

Don't get me wrong. I believe in intellectual inquiry that is open and unencumbered, free to chase the truth wherever it leads. I am deeply grateful for the education I received at the feet of learned scholars who helped me think for myself rather than simply parrot what my family, church, and culture taught me. But the benefits of a good education, however great, are *not* the point of Jesus' bold promise, "You will know the truth, and the truth will make you free" (8:32).

On what basis do I cavalierly cast aside centuries' worth of misuse of that riveting phrase? The simple fact that Jesus' bold declaration is completely dependent on the "if" clause that precedes it: "*If* you continue in my word, you are truly my disciples" (v. 31). *Then* you will know the truth, and the truth will set you free" (v. 32, NIV). The truth and freedom to which Jesus emphatically points are not truth or freedom in general, but the freedom that arises from knowing, loving, and following *him*! "*If* the Son makes you free," he tells us, "you will be free indeed!" (v. 36).

The Truth about God (8:12-29)

Jesus' gripping statement about the search for truth and freedom occurs within one of the many stories of controversy in John's

Gospel. This particular theological contest begins back in chapter 7, v. 14, and occurs in the temple (7:14; 8:20). The point/counterpoint of the debate is given dramatic expression in the story of the woman caught in adultery 7:53–8:11, and then resumes at 8:12. After Jesus proclaims himself the "light of the world," his opponents challenge what they consider an outrageous statement (8:13). As always in John's Gospel, such disputes lead Jesus to describe more fully his relationship to the Father (8:16-19).

Jesus asserts that he is not speaking for himself only, but for the Father (8:28-29). He then makes his unique, one-of-a-kind relationship to the Father (1:18; 3:16) explicit, going so far as to use the hallowed name for God, "I Am," in reference to himself: "You will die in your sins unless you believe that '*I Am*'" (8:24). (The Greek of v. 24 and v. 28 reads simply "*I Am*," not "I am *he*," as in the New Revised Standard version; see NRSV footnote c: "Gk *I am*.")

"I Am" as the definitive Hebrew name for God comes from Exodus 3:14, where the living God declares to Moses, "'I AM WHO I AM.' [God] said further, 'Thus you shall say to the Israelites, 'I AM has sent me to you.'"

John's Gospel is careful not to reduce God to Jesus, as though they were one and the same. The Father *sends* the Son (8:16, 42), the Son speaks *for* (8:28, 40, 55) and *honors* the Father (8:49-50, 54), and the Holy Spirit binds Father and Son in a communion of love (14:20-21, 23, 26). Still, in using the revered title, "I Am," in reference to himself, Jesus made a bold assertion of his divine origin (1:1-3) and nature (1:14-18; 10:30). That his enemies heard it as such is made clear by the murderous rage he inspires at the end of John 8: "'Very truly, I tell you, before Abraham was, *I Am*.' So they picked up stones to throw at him, but Jesus hid himself and went out of the temple" (8:58-59; see also 10:30-33).

In addition to the divine title, "I Am," used for Jesus, John's Gospel features seven distinctive "I Am" sayings that further explore the spiritual life Jesus gives. As the Gospel unfolds, Jesus says, (1) "I Am the bread of life" (6:35, 51), (2) "I Am the light of the world" (8:12; 9:5), (3) "I Am the gate" (10:7, 9), (4) "I Am the good shepherd" (10:11, 14), (5) "I Am the resurrection and the life" (11:25), (6) "I Am the way, the truth, and the life" (14:6), and (7) "I Am the true vine" (15:1, 5). In each case, the emphatic "I Am" means Jesus *is* the bread, *is* the light, *is* the life, and so on. Unlike every other prophet or religious teacher before and since, Jesus doesn't just preach the truth; he himself *is* the one in and through whom God's liberating truth is fleshed out in a God-breathed, fully human life (1:14, 18; 14:6).

Last year, I was blessed to attend a ministers' retreat with twenty of the most skilled, dedicated pastors I've ever met. Most of them were at or near mid-life, which meant they'd lost the cocksure confidence of youth. Many of these dear friends were whipped and exhausted and in desperate need of rest and renewal. One said, with his face wrenched by anguish, "I feel trapped in a ministry I love."

But amid the weariness and desperation, another note sounded again and again. That was the confession that through it all, God had been—and *would be*—faithful. One Episcopal rector, a fifty-ish lady who came to the ministry late, told of seeing a poster as a college student. The poster showed a vast, shimmering sea with a single, tiny boat bobbing on the surface. The caption read, "The water is so wide and my boat is so small."

"For a long time," she said, "that's the way I felt. Full of fear, I felt small and helpless. But then, as life unfolded, I discovered God was not in the boat, protecting me from the elements. And God was not in the storms, trying to do me harm. No, God was the water, holding me up."

Jesus said, "*I* am the water" (7:37-39); "*I* am the bread" (6:35); "*I* am the vine" (15:1); "*I* am the way, the truth, and the life. No one comes to the Father except through *me*" (14:6). Jesus is not merely some truth *about* God; Jesus is God's own presence, power, and peace drawing near. *That* is the truth that can set you free.

The Truth about Us (8:30-59)

In the course of Jesus' teaching in the temple, "many" see the light of God radiating through his person (v. 12) and "word" (v. 32) and "believe in him" (v. 30). Jesus counsels these new believers, "*If you continue* in my word, you are truly my disciples; *and you will know* the truth, and the truth will set you free" (vv. 31-32).

Jesus' call to "*continue*" in his word points to the forward momentum in faith. To "believe" in Jesus is not only a decision made in one's past; "believing" also means following Jesus into the future. Indeed, while John's Gospel more than any other emphasizes *believing* in Jesus, the call to *follow* Jesus is not absent. John's Gospel begins with Jesus telling Philip, "Follow me" (1:43), and ends with Jesus telling Peter the same: "Follow me" (21:9). It is not enough to "know" the truth. One must also "do" the truth (3:21; 13:17; 1 John 1:6) and "walk" in the light (12:35; 1 John 1:7).

Further, the Greek word for "know" in the phrase, "You will *know* the truth," does not signify merely intellectual knowledge, but intimate knowledge that comes through a personal relationship. Thus, those who "continue in Jesus' word" and follow him (8:12b; 10:27; 12:26) come to "know" him in a deeply personal way. It is in knowing him that one discovers "the truth that sets you free."

But while some in the crowd "believe" in Jesus (vv. 30-31), others take offense at his suggestion that they are not "free" (v. 33). Jesus answers that anyone who "commits sin is a slave to sin" (v. 34). In this Gospel, "sin" is unbelief in Jesus as God's one-of-a-kind Son (3:18b; 8:24, 37b, 43, 45; 9:40-41). Those who persist in their stubborn refusal to see the light of God in Jesus (3:19) choose an ever-deepening spiral into darkness and death. Ominously, Jesus warns that those who persist in their unbelief will "die in their sins" (v. 21, 24; 3:16b).

Thus, those who fall under the spell of sin experience an ever-deepening bondage. Far from bringing "freedom," rejecting God's truth in Jesus and "doing as one pleases" results in slavery to one's worst impulses and addictive, self-destructive behaviors. Such persons are soon "slaves to whatever masters them" (v. 34; 2 Pet 2:19b).

This deplorable state is given expression in C. S. Lewis's spiritual classic, *The Lion, the Witch, and the Wardrobe.* While in the wonder world of Narnia, Edmund falls under the spell of the White Witch. She entices him with delectable candies called Turkish delights. Each nugget of candy is scrumptious, and Edmund can't leave them alone. In fact, the more he eats, the more he wants until he is consumed by his craving. Clearly, Turkish delights are Lewis's metaphor for sin: no matter how much Edmund eats, he can never be filled. He will be enslaved but never satisfied.

By contrast, Jesus offers the bread of life, namely, himself, that fills the deepest hungers of the human heart: "I am the bread of life. Whoever comes *to me* will never be hungry" (6:35). Similarly, Jesus gives the water his indwelling Spirit that quenches the thirst of those who yearn for God (Ps 42:1-2; John 4:13-14; 7:37-29): "Whoever comes *to me* will never be thirsty" (6:35b).

Thus, one's relationship to Jesus determines one's spiritual fate: increasing light and life and freedom on the one hand, or increasing darkness, bondage, and death on the other. Those who "continue" in Jesus' word (literally, "abide" as in John 15:4, "*Abide* in me") will experience the truth that sets them free. Those who resist Jesus' truth (8:37), refusing to receive and follow his word, choose to become like those with whom Jesus does battle in John 8: stubborn, blind, enslaved, shameful, and self-destructive.

The Woman Caught in Adultery (7:53–8:11)

The story of the woman caught in adultery powerfully reveals how facing the truth about oneself in the light of Jesus' gracious, forgiving love can set one free.

The action begins as some conniving Pharisees haul an accused woman (8:3) into the temple where Jesus is teaching (v. 2). They "make her stand" before Jesus, thereby intensifying her humiliation.

"Teacher" says the ringleader, "this woman was caught in the very act of committing adultery." Given such irrefutable evidence, it seems the woman's fate is sealed: "Now in the law, Moses commanded us to stone such women. Now what do you say?" (v. 5).

An expert in the Law of Moses (5:45-47; 8:56-58; Matt 5:17-2), Jesus knows Leviticus decrees the death of the woman *and* the man involved in adultery (Lev 20:10; Deut 2:22-24). The absence of the accused man reveals this kangaroo court for the charade it is. Jesus' opponents simply want to impale him on the horns of an impossible dilemma (John 8:6).

If Jesus calls for mercy—as expected—he will be accused of disregarding Moses' Law and undermining public morality. If he concurs in stoning the woman, he will lose his well-earned reputation for love and compassion.

With the terrified woman cowering in shame, Jesus stoops down (v. 6) and begins doodling in the dirt at her accusers' feet. Some say he wrote the sins of the woman's accusers. That seems unlikely since the theological lynch mob keeps pressing Jesus for an answer (v. 7).

As the woman quakes in terror, Jesus rises to look her accusers in the eye. He levels the challenge, "Let anyone among you who is without sin be the first to throw a stone at her" (v. 7b). Remarkably, Jesus then squats back down and starts doodling again.

There is a long, noisy silence, as the wheels start turning in all those alpha male brains, poised for the kill just seconds before. The lead instigator averts his gaze from the woman to Jesus, then to the ground. Jesus' challenge yanks this man out of the rarified realms of his own self-righteousness to confront the ugly, unsavory truth. He is a manipulator and a cheat. Red-faced with embarrassment, he turns to leave.

Jesus continues to doodle while his word takes it toll. As the seconds tick by, the accusers slip away, one by one from the eldest to the youngest. Finally, just the woman—pale as a ghost—stands before Jesus.

This time he rises to look into her eyes only. "Has no one condemned you?" he asks.

"No one, sir."

"Neither do I condemn you. Go your way, and from now on do not sin again."

Once more, a central truth in John's Gospel sounds: "God did not send the Son into the world to *condemn* the world, but in order that the world might be *saved* through him" (3:17; 5:34). In the place of condemnation—whether self-condemnation or that of her accusers—Jesus offers this woman a gracious, forgiving love that will be given its supreme, world-altering expression on Jesus' cross (3:14; 8:28; 10:10-18; 12:32).

The great Southern writer, Flannery O'Connor, said being made new by God's grace was like being bitten by a snake: as the love of God courses through one's veins, one senses something is dying even as well as being reborn.

What must die in a life-changing encounter with Jesus are the lies and self-deception that hold us in bondage, whether the self-righteousness of the Pharisee that says, "I don't need saving," or the shame of the woman caught in adultery that says, "I am not worth saving." A new person is reborn with God's gracious love and presence at the center of one's being (3:3, 5-8; 4:14; 7:37-39). Such a person is no longer a "slave to sin" but a newborn child of God (1:12-13) with a place in the Son's household forever (8:35; 14:1-3).

It takes both grace and truth to set us free. In Jesus Christ, God has given both in abundant supply. That's why "if the Son makes you free, you will be free indeed!" (8:36).

1. Before studying this lesson, I thought "the truth shall make you free" meant:

____

____

____

____

2. Now I believe Jesus' statement means:

____

____

____

____

3. Jesus' writing in the dirt in John 8:6, 8 is the only time he is recorded as writing anything. What do you think he wrote?

____

____

____

____

____

4. In what way has Jesus been one or more of the following for you?

- **"I am the bread of life" (6:35, 51)**

____.

- **"I am the light of the world" (8:12; 9:5)**

____.

- **"I am the gate" (10:7, 9)**

____.

- **"I am the good shepherd" (10:11, 14)**

____.

- **"I am the resurrection and the life" (11:25)**

____.

- **"I am the way, the truth, and the life (14:6)**

____.

- **"I am the true vine" (15:1, 5)**

____.

5. What is required to "continue" or "abide" in Jesus' word? What disciplines or actions are needed?

____

____

____

____

____

6. Describe how and why sin makes slaves of people (8:34). For more on this theme, see Roman 6:15-23 and 2 Peter 2:18-9.

7. Someone has said, "The truth will make you wince before it sets you free." Can you relate a time when the truth made you "wince" before setting you free?

8. Following Jesus means accepting both God's grace for one's past—"Neither do I condemn you"—and God's grace for the future—"Go and sin no more." Discuss the distortions of discipleship that result from sacrificing either one. Compare Ephesians 2:8-19 with 2:10 and Philippians 2:12 with 2:13.

9. Relate each character in the story of the woman caught in adultery to your own experience: When do you feel accused and hopeless? When do you feel self-righteous and superior? When do you most need Jesus?

The Seven "I Am" Sayings of John's Gospel	
1	"I Am the bread of life," 6:35, 51
2	"I Am the light of the world," 8:12; 9:5
3	"I Am the gate," 10:7, 9
4	"I Am the good shepherd," 10:11, 14
5	"I Am the resurrection and the life," 11:25
6	"I Am the way, the truth, and the life," 14:6
7	"I Am the true vine," 15:1, 5

Session 7

Eternal Life

John 11:1-44

In his book, *Leadership Jazz* (New York: Currency Doubleday, 1992), Max De Pree tells a story about his granddaughter, Zoe. Born prematurely, Zoe weighed only one pound, seven ounces at birth. She was so small Max could slip his wedding ring over her hand and slide it all the way up to her shoulder. The doctors didn't expect the tiny preemie to survive. Connected to a respirator, two IVs, and a feeding tube, she was a pitiful sight.

Zoe's biological father abandoned the family a month before her birth, so Max was asked to stand in as a substitute. A wise nurse told him to visit as much as possible and rub Zoe's body with the tip of his finger. While touching her, he was to speak softly and lovingly. It was crucial, said the nurse, for the baby to connect the voice and the touch. Perhaps because the little one did, she lived. That is how she got her name, "Zoe," the Greek word for life.

Greek, the original language of the New Testament, has two words for life: *bios*, from which we get our word "*bio*-logy," and *zoe*, referring to spiritual life. In John's Gospel, Jesus promises those who trust in him *zoe* life. To be sure, zoe life means life that lasts forever, but it means far more than that. In fact, just living forever could be a fate worse than death, depending on the quality of one's life and the kind of person one is.

In the book of Genesis, when Adam and Eve are expelled from the garden, cherubim armed with a flaming sword are posted at the gate (Gen 3:24). The point of securing Eden is to keep Adam and Eve from slipping back into the garden, eating of the tree of life, and thereby condemning themselves to life forever in their fallen state.

Before they or we are fit to live forever, we need to receive the God-breathed, Spirit-filled life Jesus came to give. *That* is the heart of Jesus' bold promise in John 3:16. Not just the promise of life *forever,* but the possibility of a rich, abundant, God-blessed life *now*: "For God so loved the world, God gave the one-of-a-kind Son that whoever trusts in him might not perish, but have *zoe* life!" (3:16).

Life Abundant, Life Eternal

The English word "life" (Greek *zoe*) occurs more than three dozen times in John's Gospel, and the verb "to live" (Greek *zen*) occurs more than a dozen times. But more important than the word count is the way *zoe* appears at key points in the narrative. Indeed, this Gospel begins with the promise of life—"In him was *life,* and the *life* was the light of all people" (1:5)—and ends on the same note: "These [things] are written so that you may come to believe that Jesus is the Messiah, the Son of God, and that through believing you may have *life* in his name" (20:31).

Between these "book ends" of the Gospel of John, Jesus repeatedly promises eternal life to those who believe in him (3:15-16; 3:36; 5:21, 24; 10:28; 17:3; 20:31). Jesus calls himself the bread of *life* (6:35, 48), the water of *life* (4:14; 7:37-39), the words of *life* (6:63, 68), and the light of *life* (1:4-5, 9; 8:12.) In John 11:25, Jesus declares himself the "resurrection and the *life,*" anticipating not only the raising of Lazarus but Jesus' own death and resurrection to which John's Gospel will soon turn (11:53).

While the terms "life" and "eternal life" are used synonymously in this Gospel, the adjective "eternal" clarifies the nature of spiritual or *zoe* life. Yes, "eternal life" lasts "forever," but "eternal" also points to the *quality* of new life that Jesus gives. "Eternal life" is "life from above" where God is (1:51; 3:12-13, 31; 6:62; 8:23; 19:11; 20:17), a new, Spirit-breathed life given those who trust in Jesus as God's Son (3:3, 5).

Thus, Jesus gives the gift of eternal life, a life that begins *now* (3:16; 10:10) and lasts *forever* (10:28).

A Crisis in Bethany (11:1-16)

The story of Lazarus's raising gives unforgettable expression to the conviction that Jesus is the Lord of life.

The story begins with bitter disappointment. Three of Jesus' dearest friends, Martha, Mary, and Lazarus (vv. 2-3, 5), are in crisis: Lazarus is deathly ill. The worried sisters send an urgent message to Jesus: "Lord, he whom you love is ill" (v. 3).

Instead of hastening to the aid of his beloved friends, Jesus stays put and makes the pronouncement, "This illness does not lead to death; rather it is for God's *glory* so that the Son of God may be *glorified* through it" (v. 4).

"Glory" is a code word in John's Gospel for the presence and power of God, manifest in Jesus (1:18; 2:11; 12:41, 43; 17:22, 24). Jesus is reassuring his disciples that the crisis in Bethany (v. 1) is an opportunity for God's glory in him to shine. Though John is quick to reassure the reader that Jesus "loves" Martha, Mary, and Lazarus (v. 5), it seems a strange love indeed since Jesus does not rush to his friend's aid.

Clearly, Jesus does not operate with a conventional definition of death. He tells his disciples, "This illness does not lead to *death*" (v. 4), then waits two days until Lazarus indeed dies. But for Jesus, the physical death of a believer is no more threatening or final than "sleep" (vv. 11, 14), a tender euphemism for death used elsewhere in the New Testament (Mark 5:39; Acts 7:60; 1 Cor 15:6; and 1 Thess 4:13).

In addition, one can be physically alive, possessing *bios*, but completely lacking in *zoe*—the God-breathed spiritual life Jesus offers (8:21, 24). By contrast, those who trust in Jesus as God's Son pass from spiritual death into spiritual life (5:24; 8:51-52) and will "never" die (11:26; 6:50) or "perish" (3:16; 10:28).

The Resurrection and the Life (11:17-26)

After waiting for Lazarus's death, Jesus travels to Bethany. Upon arriving, he learns Lazarus has been in the tomb four days. The mention of "four days," noted twice in the text (vv. 17, 39), is significant. According to traditional expectations of the period, the spirit of a dead person hovered near the body for three days. After three days, any hope of life was gone. "Four days" means Lazarus is absolutely, irrevocably *dead.*

Meanwhile, some of the mourners notify Martha and Mary that Jesus has finally arrived. Upon hearing this, Martha goes to meet Jesus while Mary continues to grieve in private (vv. 19-20). Martha's words carry the sting of accusation: "Lord, if you had *been here*, my brother would not have died" (v. 21). Then she adds a plea borne of desperation, "And *even now* I know God will give you whatever you ask" (v. 22).

Jesus responds with words that sound like a pious cliché: "Your brother will rise again" (v. 23). Martha summons the faith to acknowledge—even if by rote—the truth of what Jesus says: "I know that he will rise again in the resurrection on the last day" (v. 24). But as Martha is about to discover, Jesus is not talking about raising Lazarus in the "sweet by and by." Jesus is talking about the here and now.

In the fifth of his "I Am" sayings, Jesus declares emphatically, "*I* am the resurrection and the life. Those who believe in me, even though they die, will live, and everyone who lives and believes in me will never die" (vv. 25-26). Once again Jesus talks about death in a literal, physical sense, as well as a spiritual or metaphorical sense: Those who believe in him will die physically—"Even though they *die*" (v. 25b)—but they will not die spiritually. They will "live" (v. 26) because their life with God continues (10:28-29). Thus, in a real sense, those who trust in Jesus "never die" (v. 26), for while the body may die (or "sleep," v. 11), the person himself or herself lives on in God's nearer presence (14:1).

In Jesus, the "last day" (v. 24) of resurrection is *now*: "I *am* the resurrection and life," he proclaims. Thus, the eternal life Jesus offers begins in the present—"He who has the Son has *zoe* life!" (3:16, 36a)—and continues forever: "I give them eternal life, and they will never perish. No one will snatch them out of my hand" (10:28; see also 5:28-29; 6:39, 44, 54). Because of the new life, the eternal life, the presence and peace of the living God that Jesus gives those who trust in him, physical death has lost its power to terrify God's children.

Charles Kingsley, an Anglican clergyman in Victorian England, spent his final months in a hospital for the terminally ill. His wife was a patient in the same hospital. Since these two were in separate rooms, they kept in touch by sending notes. One day, Kingsley's wife sent a message written in trembling script that read, "My darling, is it cowardly of me to tremble before the unseen reality of death?"

The great man of faith wrote back, "Do not be afraid! It will not be dark, because God is light. There will be no loneliness for Christ will be there."

The book of Hebrews says Jesus can free "those who all their lives were held in slavery by the fear of death" (2:15). Lazarus was the first of many to learn how true that is.

Do You Believe This? (11:27-38)

After proclaiming himself the resurrection and the life, Jesus asks Martha, "Do you believe this?" She answers by asserting her faith in *him* (v. 27), even if she cannot yet fathom the extent of the triumph over death Jesus is about to win (v. 39).

Next, Martha calls her more reserved sister to Jesus' side (v. 28). When Mary reaches Jesus, she bows reverently but does not spare him the same biting accusation leveled by her sister: "Lord, if you had been here, my brother would not have died" (v. 32, v. 21). When Jesus sees Mary weeping at his feet—and the weeping of the other mourners—he is "greatly disturbed in spirit and deeply moved" (v. 33).

While Jesus earlier appears almost nonchalant about the death of his beloved friend (vv. 3, 15), here we see him deeply grieved by Martha and Mary's anguish and the ugly reality of death. Indeed, three times the text notes Jesus that is profoundly moved by the death of Lazarus and the grief it brings (vv. 33, 35, 38). For Jesus, as for us, the death of a dear loved one or friend hurts. It hurts a *lot*! Paul rightly called death "the last enemy" (1 Cor 15:26). Well-intentioned Christians, eager to comfort the bereaved, would do well to ponder Jesus' example. Often the best comfort one can offer the bereaved is to share another's tears.

Watching the Savior tremble and quake before that tomb, his face wet with tears, we realize that the talk of "glory" with which this story began (v. 4) was not a cheap cliché of comfort. In this Gospel, the supreme revelation of God's glory in Jesus will radiate from the cross (3:13-14; 12:32; 17:1). By waiting for Lazarus to die and then raising him—rather than healing Lazarus at the outset—Jesus creates a sensation (12:9-11) that ensures his own death (11:53). Yet despite his enemies' growing resolve to eliminate him, Jesus still comes to Lazarus's tomb. Yes, he comes in his own sweet time, but still he comes because he has spoken and will soon live the truth, "Greater love has no man than this that he lay down his *life for his friends*" (15:13; 11:3, 5).

In John 10, Jesus speaks of himself as the Good Shepherd who must lay down his life for his sheep (10:11); in John 11, Jesus raises Lazarus to new life. Clearly, these two chapters foreshadow the death and resurrection of Jesus.

What does it say about God that Jesus, God's beloved Son, shares not only our tears but even our death in order to give us eternal life now and forever? John 3:16 proves a costly promise to keep.

Lazarus, Come Out! (11:39-44)

As Jesus stands before Lazarus's tomb, hewn from a rocky hillside, he commands that the round millstone be rolled back from the door. Martha is horrified since Lazarus has been dead for four days and there is already a stench (v. 39). She considers the situation hopeless (vv. 17, 39).

Jesus challenges Martha yet again, once more promising the revelation of God's glory (v. 40), and the gravestone is rolled away (v. 41). Then Jesus prays aloud so the crowd will know this mighty work arises from no power in himself (John 8:28b-29, 54), but from God the "Father" who sent him (John 5:23). After the prayer, Jesus cries out in a loud voice, "Lazarus, come out!" and the newly raised man emerges, his burial wrappings still clinging to him: "Unbind him," Jesus commands, "and let him go!" (vv. 43-44).

It is a shocking and stupendous ending to what everyone thought was a hopeless situation. Which, of course, it was—until Jesus showed up.

In the mines of north Africa, one can still see messages scribbled by second- and third-century Christians. These believers were sentenced to labor until death in those dank, dark mines because they confessed Christ, rather than Caesar, as Lord.

Branded on the brow with a red-hot iron, eyes gouged out and chained so they could not stand upright, they faced a slow, grueling death. Yet the inscription they most often etched on the walls of those caves were the words, "*Vita, Vita, Vita,*" Latin for "Life, Life, Life." Not even the savagery and ruin of their cruel fate could silence the confession that Jesus Christ was the Lord of life.

Jesus *is* the resurrection and the life. No matter how dire one's circumstances, he has the power to give new life, hope, and vitality *now.* No matter how bleak one's future, he has the power to give new life *forever.*

As Lazarus's tomb—and soon Jesus' own tomb—make emphatically clear, Jesus Christ is the Lord of *life, life, life*!

1. Can you relate a time when, like Martha and Mary, you felt ignored and forgotten by Jesus? Did Jesus finally show up? If so, when and how?

2. How might the realization that "eternal life" brings *quality* of life, as well as *duration* of life, change your understanding of faith and discipleship?

3. The "eternal life" Jesus gives is called "abundant life" in John 10:10. Drawing on the story of the wedding at Cana (2:1-11; 3:34b) and the story of Lazarus's raising, describe some of the elements of "abundant life."

4. Can you relate an experience where God was "glorified" through illness? Through grief? Through death?

5. Some Christians believe showing grief and heartbreak reveals a lack of faith. Where does that idea come from, especially given Jesus' own grief at Lazarus's tomb (vv. 33, 35, 38)?

6. In what ways is "sleep" (KJV, NIV) an apt metaphor for those who have died in faith (1 Cor 15:6; 1 Thess 4:13)?

7. In many ways, the story of Lazarus is a story about Jesus' power to give eternal life *now* (3:15-16, 36; 4:14; 5:21-26; 6:47-48; 10:10; 11:25; 17:3). Can you name some of the "little resurrections" in your life that point to the great resurrection yet to be?

8. When Lazarus emerges from his tomb, Jesus commands, "Unbind him and let him go" (v. 44). Of what, besides death, has Jesus set Lazarus free? What "grave clothes" are you wearing that you'd like for Jesus to strip away?

Session 8

Love

John 13:1-20, 31-35; 17:20-26

In fall 2004, I was blessed to attend a meeting of the European Baptist Federation in Lebanon. While there, I met a remarkable young man named Samer. A Palestinian, Samer grew up in Lebanon a devout Muslim. In fact, he was so serious about his faith that he was studying to become a Muslim holy man. He taught in the mosque and called the crowds to prayer, singing over the loud speakers mounted in the mosque's minaret.

One night Samer attended an open-air meeting organized by a Lebanese Christian leader and Cooperative Baptist Fellowship missionary. At first, Samer was hostile to the gospel. When given a New Testament, he threw it to the ground. But as Samer returned to the evangelistic meetings night after night, a new experience of God's grace began stirring in his heart. Moved by the good news of Jesus, Samer became a Christian.

After his conversion, Samer was kidnapped twice by extremists. His family disowned him and his life was threatened. Eventually, Christian friends whisked him away from the refugee camps to a safer area. Today, Samer is a street evangelist in downtown Beirut, trying to win to Jesus all who will listen.

In his pocket, Samer carries a photograph of himself washing the feet of a Jewish Christian he met at a retreat center in Cyprus. That amazing photograph of a former Muslim washing the feet of a Jew, his sworn enemy, is a powerful testament to the transforming power of Jesus' love. "No one else could do that but Jesus," Samer says, pointing to the picture and beaming. "Only Jesus."

The night before his death, Jesus took a basin of water and washed the feet of his disciples. Then he told them—and all who would believe in his name—"I give you a new commandment, that you love one another. Just as I have loved you, you also should love one another. By this everyone will know that you are my disciples, if you have love for one another" (13:34-35).

A Love Lavished: Washing the Disciples' Feet (13:1-11)

The riveting story of Jesus washing his disciples' feet follows shortly after the raising of Lazarus. Indeed, the raising of Lazarus is the continental divide in the Gospel of John. After this climatic event, all the action flows toward the cross (11:53).

Immediately on the heels of Lazarus's raising, a grateful Mary anoints Jesus' feet with costly ointment, a preparation, says Jesus, for his burial (12:1-11). Next, an ecstatic Passover crowd receives Jesus into Jerusalem (12:12-19), its enthusiasm fueled by the "sign" of Lazarus (v. 18). During the festival, some Greeks seek an audience with Jesus (12:20-26). Perhaps because their interest signifies the spiritual hunger of the larger world (3:16-17), Jesus determines "the hour has come for the Son of man to be glorified" (12:23), a reference to his death (vv. 24, 31-33). Chapter 12 ends with an important summary of the key truths of John's Gospel (12:44-50), and then the curtain closes on the first half of the Gospel.

When the curtain rises on act 2, the second half of the Gospel (chs. 13–21), Jesus arranges a "last supper" with his disciples. This is not the Passover meal, as in the first three Gospels (Matt 26:17-30; Mark 14:12-26; Luke 22:7-23), but occurs "before" the Passover (13:1). Fittingly, in John's Gospel, Jesus is crucified as the Passover lambs are slain (19:14), since Jesus is the Lamb of God who takes away the sins of the world (1:29, 35). In fact, an account of the Lord's Supper does not appear in John's Gospel, though the meaning of the Lord's Supper is explored in the story of the feeding of the five thousand (6:35-59). Perhaps knowing his readers were thoroughly familiar with the story of the Lord's Supper, John put his emphasis elsewhere, namely, on the example of Jesus' loving, sacrificial service (13:1-5).

Jesus' shocking act of washing his disciples' feet violated the rules of decorum in the first-century world. Ordinarily, a servant was given the menial task of washing the dirty feet of travelers arriving after travel over dusty roads. Jesus' poor, ragtag band had no such servants, and none of the disciples was about to take this uninviting duty upon himself. Ever jostling for position (Mark 10:35-45; Matt 23:8-12), Jesus' disciples sat with dirty feet and defiant spirits, waiting for someone else to make the first move. Finally, someone did.

Jesus quietly rose from his seat and poured water into a basin. When Jesus knelt before the first disciple, taking dirty feet in his hands, a stunned, awkward silence fell over the room. The disciples watched in disbelief as Jesus gently took each man's feet in turn, splashed the feet with water, and washed the grit and grime away.

Why would Jesus stoop to such an indignity? "Because," John's Gospel answers, "he loved them *to the end*" (v. 1). Jesus' love reached all the way to the dirty, ugly extremities of his followers' bodies and, yes, to the dirty, ugly extremities of their lives. Even when they were completely unlovable, he loved them still. Supremely at his cross, he took their soiled, broken lives in his hands, banished their shame, and brought cleansing, forgiveness, and new life.

Jesus' washing of his disciples' feet powerfully foreshadows the love lavished on his cross. The reader is told at the beginning of the story that the time had come for Jesus to "depart from this world and go to the Father" (vv. 1-3). Further, the same verbs used for the Good Shepherd *laying down* and *taking up* his life (10:11, 15, 17-18) are used in chapter 13 of Jesus *taking off* (v. 4) and *putting on* his robe (v. 12). When Peter protests Jesus' shocking gesture, Jesus tells Peter he must wait until "later" to understand fully (v. 8). Only in light of all that is about to happen, namely Jesus' crucifixion and resurrection, will the disciples be able to fathom the depths of God's love in Jesus (v. 19).

During my college years, a poster in my dorm room depicted Jesus on his cross. Beneath the stark, moving image was the caption, "I asked Jesus how much he loved me. 'This much,' he answered. Then he spread his arms open wide and died for me."

Recently, the contemporary Christian group, Casting Crowns, stirred this memory for me with a song on their album *The Altar and the Door* (2007). The evocative song, "East to West," is built around the psalmist's confession, "As far as the east is from the west, so far [God] removes our sins from us" (Ps 103:12).

"Jesus, can you show me just how far the east is from the west," the singer pleads, "'cause I can't bear to see the man I've been come rising up in me again." Then, with deep feeling, he continues, "In the arms of your mercy I find rest—'cause you know just how far the east is from the west—*from one scarred hand to the other.*"

In each new generation, the startling promise of the gospel sounds anew: the gracious God who draws near in Jesus Christ already knows and has forgiven every ugly, unseemly truth about us. How do we know this? Because at Jesus' cross, the living God took our dirty, soiled lives in hand and loved us "to the end" (13:3; 19:30).

A Love Evoked: A New Commandment (13:12-20, 31-35)

The reckless, extravagant love of God in Jesus Christ is so startling and unprecedented that no ordinary word for "love" will do. Consequently, the early Christians effectively coined a new word to describe the character of God's consuming, unconditional love: the word *agape.*

Ancient Greek had four primary words for love: (1) *eros,* the word for romantic attraction, (2) *philia,* the word for friendship love, (3) *storge,* or family love, and (4) *Agape,* a general word for love or affection. However, in New Testament usage, the writers used the word *agape* in such a distinctive way that it effectively became a new word that refers to the unconditional, uncompromising, unrelenting love of God.

Agape love is at the heart of John's Gospel and the New Testament letters bearing John's name. This love compels God to send God's one and only Son to bring light and life in a dark, foreboding world (3:16). Further, Jesus loves "his own" (13:1) as the Father loves him (3:25; 5:20), and through faith in Jesus, the believer shares in the communion of love that flows between God the Father and God the Son in the presence and power of the Holy Spirit (14:21, 23; 16:27; 17:26).

But the agape love of God is not just an *experience* of the believer, but Jesus' *expectation* of the believer. After washing his disciples' feet, Jesus proclaims, "I have set you an example, that you also should do as I have done to you" (13:15). Jesus' brand of loving, sacrificial service is to characterize his followers: "If I, your Lord and Teacher, have washed your feet, you also ought to wash one another's feet" (v. 14).

In one of the companion letters to John's Gospel, the letter of 1 John, the writer says, "We know love by this, that [Christ] laid down his life for us—*and we ought to lay down our lives for one another*" (1 John 3:16; John 15:13). What does it mean to "lay down one's life for another"? It means to "lay down" whatever is getting in the way of loving another person as Jesus would love him or her: our wounded pride, sense of privilege, fear of involvement, busyness, *whatever*. As Jesus laid aside his robe—and his eternal life with God!—to take upon himself the form of a servant (Phil 2:5-11), so Christians are called to follow him in the way of sacrificial, loving service.

In the movie *Bruce Almighty*, Jim Carrey plays a frustrated television reporter named Bruce Nolan. Bruce is granted Godlike abilities but discovers that compelling displays of power cannot change the world. Only small miracles of love, offered up day by day, can do that.

"You want a miracle?" God says to Bruce, the frustrated television reporter and would-be savior. "If you want to *see* a miracle, *be* a miracle."

In John's Gospel—as in Matthew, Mark, and Luke—many look for a "sign" to prove Jesus' divine authority. For most, such a sign means an indisputable display of God's power. Jesus, however, points to a different kind of sign, namely the loving care and service present in his disciples: "*Be* a miracle! Love one another as I have loved you!" (13:34).

That They May Be One (17:20-26)

Lest all this talk of loving service get lost in a sentimental haze, John's Gospel frankly acknowledges that loving others—even fellow church members and friends—can be a daunting challenge.

The first such acknowledgment comes as the Last Supper unfolds: the betrayal of Judas (13:2, 10-11). Because Judas has not allowed himself to be "cleansed" by Jesus' word (15:3; 17:17, 19) and love (13:10-11), he falls victim to Satan's ploys (13:27), forsaking Jesus' light for the "night" (13:30) where evil beckons.

The second and in some ways even more profound acknowledgment of the difficulty of loving others is found in Jesus' prayer, recorded in John 17 (the setting is still the Last Supper). One could argue that this prayer—the longest prayer of Jesus in the New Testament—might rightly be called the *Lord's* Prayer. For here Jesus is not just teaching or modeling prayer for others (Luke 11:1-4; Matt 6:7-15); he is praying for himself (17:1-5), for his disciples (17:6-19), and for his church—those who will believe because of the disciples' witness (17:20-26).

In the third movement of his prayer (17:20-26), Jesus prays that those who believe in him may be "one," so the world may believe in

God's Son and the new life he brings (vv. 21-23). Jesus yearns to be present in the believing community as the Father is present in him (vv. 22, 26). Indeed, Jesus' teaching in chapter 13—"By this will everyone know you are my disciples, if you have love for one another" (v. 35)—here becomes his earnest prayer.

Sadly, in many times and places, Jesus' prayer has gone unanswered. A *Newsweek* article titled "A Christian by Any Other Name" reported on a trend where many are jettisoning the name "Christian" for the designation "follower of Jesus." This trend is fueled in part by a reaction against the divisive culture wars some Christians in America have waged around issues such as abortion and homosexuality. Whereas in Antioch, the first believers were called "Christians" because they reminded others of Jesus (Acts 11:26), today some reject that label because so many self-professed Christians remind people of someone or something *other* than Jesus! (Lisa Miller, "A Christian by Any Other Name," *Newsweek*, 7 March 2009, http://www.newsweek.com/id/188198)

One might hope that if everyone just loved Jesus, all our differences and disputes would magically disappear, but that wasn't true in New Testament times and it isn't true today. Even in the churches of John, there were serious factions and divisions (1 John 2:4, 9, 11; 3:18-19, 22-23; 4:1-3, 20-21; 2 John 7-11; 3 John 9-10). And the nasty rivalries tearing apart the church at Corinth, Paul's most troubled church (1 Cor 1:10-17; 3:1-4; 4:6-7; 6:1-13; 8:9-13; 10:23-30; 11:17-22, 27-32; 12:14-26; 13:1-3), make the average congregation today look like a convocation of Peaceniks! If the unity Jesus yearned for, prayed for, and died for were easily achieved, his prayer would have been answered long ago.

Still, many Christians and churches *do* exemplify the spirit of sacrificial love Jesus taught and embodied. The depth of their experience of Jesus' grace empowers such disciples to be gracious and loving toward others. According to Jesus, such followers are far more than his *servants*; they are his *friends* (John 15:14-15).

A little girl was drawing with crayons in Sunday school. Looking over her shoulder, the teacher asked, "What are you drawing?"

"I'm drawing God."

"God!" said the teacher. "But no one knows what God looks like!"

Unruffled, the child answered, "They will when I'm done."

Pray that the lives of those who know, love, and follow Jesus will draw such a picture of God.

1. Imagine having Jesus take your feet in his hands. What do you feel as he approaches? What is it like to feel his hands grip your bare feet? What do you say? What do you do?

2. What did Jesus mean by saying, "If I, your Lord and Teacher, have washed your feet, you also ought to wash one another's feet" (13:14)? What does it mean to "wash" one another's feet?

3. Read the Wikipedia article on "Servant Leadership" (http://en.wikipedia.org/wiki/Servant_leadership). In what ways is Jesus' washing his disciples' feet an example of what is today called "Servant Leadership"?

4. John 13:3 says that Jesus—knowing "he had come *from God* and was going *to God*"—took the towel of service upon himself. What frees us to be servant leaders like Jesus?

5. Ponder Jesus' action as an acted parable, not just of the cross, but of the entire drama of the coming to earth of God's eternal Son (1:1-18; Phil 2:5-11).

6. Talk about all the ways the word "love" is used in English. Create a simile to describe the unique character of God's *agape*-style love: God's agape-*agape* love is like:

but *not* like:

7. In John 15, Jesus proclaims that those who follow him in the way of sacrificial service are not merely "servants," but "friends" (15:12-15). What is the significance of that distinction? How does it feel to be Jesus' "friend" instead of just his "servant"?

8. What have some Christians done to make people want to reject the label "Christian" altogether? What are some positive examples of Christians in your church or community loving others as Jesus has loved them?

____

____

____

____

____

9. Search the Cooperative Baptist Fellowship website (www.thefellowship.info) or the sites of other Christian organizations and identify some of the ways this movement of God's people seeks to "be Christ's presence in the world." What are some of the ways your church strives to be the presence of Christ in the world? What about you?

____

____

____

____

____

Session 9

Paraclete/Abide

John 14:1–16:33

When I was a young pastor, just starting out, I was blessed with a beloved mentor named Tibor Chikes. Tibor was a Hungarian Reformed pastor who immigrated to America in the late 1950s. For years, he taught pastoral counseling at Wesley Theological Seminary in Washington, DC.

Tibor was a brilliant professor and academic, yet he radiated a vital, childlike faith in Jesus Christ. I longed for the integration of head and heart I saw in him. One day I asked Tibor about the calm I sensed at the center of his being.

He told a harrowing tale about the years after the Second World War when the Soviets occupied his native Hungary. Driven by atheistic zeal, the Soviets were intent on crushing all resistance. Christian leaders like Tibor were considered Public Enemy Number One.

One day all the pastors in Budapest were rounded up and marched to a city many miles distant. As they marched through deep snow in the dead of winter, several pastors died from exposure, and all were infected with despair. Then, on the third day of the march, a drunken corporal told the prisoners to line up with their faces against a brick wall. A machine gun began firing at their backs.

Tibor recalled the moment. "As I stood there shivering in the snow, I knew I was going to die. And I thought of the absurdity of this death, stripped of everything I had ever known or valued. It was doubtful my family would even be told of my execution.

"Then suddenly, a great peace swept over me, even as I heard the machine gun fire drawing nearer. For I knew that in that moment, though everything else had been taken away—*Christ was in me and I was in Christ*—and death was powerless to sever the bond between us."

Eventually, the machine gun fire subsided, and Tibor's life was spared. The Russian's intent was merely to terrorize the prisoners, not kill them all. But as Tibor took up the dreaded march once again, he was a man transformed. Now he knew that while everything else could be snatched away in an instant, he belonged to Christ—and Christ belonged to him—*forever*!

As the end drew near for Jesus, he told his disciples, "In the world you face persecution. But take courage; I have conquered the world!" (16:33). It was and is a precious promise. In every generation, believers find that the promise proves true when they need it most.

Trouble All Around (14:1-27)

As Jesus instructs his disciples in the upper room during the Last Supper (chs. 13–17), the theme of his discourse turns to trouble: "Do not let your hearts be *troubled.* Believe in God, believe also in me" (14:1). This is a lot to ask because trouble is closing in on all sides. Indeed, after Judas departs to betray his Lord (13:10-11, 21, 26-30), Jesus declares that he is about to go where his disciples cannot follow (13:33, 36-38). They have every reason to be *troubled.*

Indeed, Jesus himself is no stranger to "trouble." He is "troubled" at Mary's weeping over the death of her brother, Lazarus (11:33). (The verb "troubled" is translated "greatly disturbed" in the NRSV, but it is the same Greek verb as in John 14:1.) Jesus is "troubled" as he contemplates his impending suffering and death (12:27). Jesus is "troubled" at the painful reality of Judas's betrayal (13:21).

For Jesus as for those who love him, feeling troubled is not uncommon in an often difficult world. That Jesus experienced such trouble—especially in this Gospel that so forcefully presents his divine Sonship—is a sign of his true humanity.

But for the believer, as for Jesus, such "trouble" is but a way station in the journey of faith; it is not one's final destination. Even in the hard times, amid the most terrible pressures imaginable, there can be incredible calm because of the gift Jesus gives: the gift of the Holy Spirit, the gift of *himself.*

The Paraclete

As the disciples reel from the news that Jesus is about to leave them, Jesus makes a beautiful and beloved promise: "In my Father's house there are many dwelling places. If it were not so, would I have told you that I go to prepare a place for you? And if I go and prepare a place for you, I will come again and take you to myself, so that where I am, there you may be also." (14:2-3)

Because Jesus lives, those who trust in him shall live also, now and forevermore (11:25-26.) Death is but a passageway to that most glorious of destinations: the Father's House. There the believer will continue to know a rich, full life in Jesus' presence.

When Thomas protests that the disciples don't fully grasp "the place" or "the way" Jesus is going, Jesus answers with one of the pivotal truths John's Gospel: "*I* am the way, the truth, and the life. No one comes to the Father except through me" (14:6). This leads to yet another exploration of the theme so central to this Gospel: in Jesus, God's one-of-a-kind Son, the Eternal God whom Jesus calls the "Father" draws near (vv. 7-14).

Because of Jesus' unique relationship to the heavenly Father, he can promise the most precious of gifts: the gift of "another Advocate" (14:16)—namely, the Holy Spirit (v. 26)—who will be with the disciples forever. The Holy Spirit is *another* Advocate because Jesus is the first (1 John 2:1). Jesus has stood by the disciples, guiding, encouraging, and empowering them. Now as Jesus' physical presence is withdrawn, the Holy Spirit will fill the crucial role of Advocate and Friend.

Throughout his upper room discourse, Jesus explores the nature and work of the Holy Spirit whom he calls the *Paraclete.* "Paraclete"—the English transliteration of the Greek word *Parakletos*—is John's special word for the Holy Spirit (14:26). In the New Testament, this word is found only in the writings attributed to John. Meaning literally "one called alongside," a *paraclete* might be a witness or advocate speaking in one's defense in court, or an expert called upon to give advice or guidance.

English Bible translations offer a wide variety of words for the *Paraclete* we know as the Holy Spirit: Counselor, Guide, Advocate, Comforter, Teacher, Helper, and Friend among them. However, no single English word captures all the facets of the Paraclete's work as described in John 14–16. Consequently, it is probably best to preserve the richness and distinctiveness of John's title by using the English transliteration of the Greek: *Paraclete.*

The Paraclete's Work (chs. 14–16)

Five passages in John 14–16 explore the work of the Paraclete. Sometimes called the "Paraclete Sayings," these passages are (1) 14:16-17; (2) 14:25-26; (3) 15:26-27; (4) 16:7-11; and (5) 16:12-15.

The first and most crucial work of the Paraclete is to bring Jesus near: "I will not leave you orphaned," Jesus promises his disciples. "*I* will come to you" (14:18). On the far side of Jesus' suffering and death, he will come to his disciples first in his resurrection appearances (14:19-20; 16:16-22). Then, following Jesus' return to the Father (14:28-29; 16:17b; 20:17), he will also return to believers in the spiritual presence of the Paraclete, the Holy Spirit, whom the Father will send in Jesus' name (v. 26). The Paraclete will "teach" and "remind" believers of all that Jesus has said (14:25-26). As a result, they will know peace even in a world of trouble (14:27).

But the Paraclete is not just a *reminder* of Jesus; the Paraclete is the *real presence* of Jesus. To those who keep Jesus' commandments (14:21) and word (vv. 23-23), thereby demonstrating their loyalty and love, Jesus makes the promise, "*I* will love them and reveal *myself* to them" (v. 21). Both Jesus and the Father will come and "make our home" with those who love him (v. 23).

Here we find ourselves wading into the deep waters of the Trinity. While the Father, Son, and Holy Spirit can be separated for purposes of discussion, the loving communion at the heart of the triune God can never be broken. Hence, for the believer, to know the Spirit is to know Jesus is to know the Father. It is impossible to fathom the mystical depth of love between the Father, Son, and Holy Spirit (the Paraclete) in John 14–16 without some notion of God's Three-in-Oneness.

The confidence that animates John 14–16, and indeed the entire Gospel of John, is that the risen Jesus can be as real and vivid in believers' lives today as he was in the lives of those blessed to know him in the flesh. Indeed, Jesus says, "it is to your *advantage* that I go away, for if I do not go away, the Advocate will not come to you; but if I go, I will send him to you" (16:7). The Paraclete allows Jesus to be present to all believers in all times and places. The Paraclete extends Jesus' mission and multiplies the effectiveness of his work (14:12b; 17:18; 20:21-23). Because of the presence of the risen Jesus, whom the Paraclete brings near, those who have "not seen" Jesus can be as blessed—perhaps even more blessed—than those who have seen him (20:29; 1 Pet 1:8).

Years ago, in a world before cell phones or even dedicated land lines, an operator was needed to connect two parties wishing to speak by telephone. There was a slight delay as the operator made the necessary connections during which he or she might say, "I'm trying to connect you." Then, when the connection was made, the operator faded out of the conversation.

In many ways, the Paraclete's work as described in John 14–16 is like that: the Paraclete acts to create a connection, a living communion, between Jesus and the believer (14:25-27; 15:26-27; 16:12-15).

In addition, the Paraclete continues Jesus' work of revealing God's truth; three times the Paraclete is called the "Spirit of Truth" (14:17; 15:26; 16:13): (1) the Paraclete *reveals* God's truth, as did Jesus (14:16-17); (2) the Paraclete *teaches* God's truth, as did Jesus (14:25-26); (3) the Paraclete *convicts* the world of *un*truth—of sin and evil—as did Jesus (16:7-11). The Paraclete brings home the truth of Jesus' word and presence amid the ever-changing circumstances of life (16:12-15). Again, the Paraclete is *another* Advocate (14:16; 1 John 2:1) because his work is so much like Jesus' own.

"Shall I tell you," asked David Livingstone upon his return from missionary service in Africa, "what sustained me amidst the toil and hardship, and loneliness of my exiled life? It was the promise, 'Lo, I am with you always, even unto the end'" (see Matt 28:20b). The Paraclete takes Jesus' precious promise and brands it upon every believing heart.

The Gift the Paraclete Makes Possible: "Abiding" (15:1-17)

The Paraclete's work makes possible an intimate union between Jesus and the believer, a union given vivid expression in Jesus' teaching about the vine and the branches. As no vine can long survive apart from a vital union to the branch that sustains its life, even so the believer can thrive and grow only as he or she is "in" Jesus and Jesus is "in" the believer (15:4). "Apart from me," Jesus solemnly warns, "you can do nothing" (v. 5b).

The word Jesus uses to describe the Spirit-breathed (3:3, 7-8; 20:22), life-giving union between himself and the believer is "abide." Ten times in only seven verses (15:4-10), Jesus urges his disciples to "abide" in him, variously translated as "indwell," "reside," and "live." It is as the Paraclete, the Holy Spirit, "abides" in the believer (14:16-17) that the believer, in turn, "abides" in Jesus (15:4-5). Such "abiding" points to the deeply personal relationship between Jesus and those who love and trust him.

How does the believer *abide* in Jesus even as Jesus *abides* within the believer? First by knowing, meditating upon, and obeying the *word of Jesus* (14:23-24; 15:3, 7, 20, 25; 17:6, 14, 17). The word of Jesus—the teaching and truth of Jesus—shapes and "prunes" the lives of those who follow him. In pruning, the cut branch or limb is driven back to its source, thereby becoming more vital and strong. In the spiritual arena as in the garden, pruning is essential to growth and fruitfulness (15:2b, 16b).

Second, the believer abides in Jesus through the *power of prayer.* Jesus stands ready to give believers whatever they need to follow him (15:7, 16b; 14:13-14; 16:23-24). However, the promise, "Ask for whatever you wish, and it will be done for you" (15:7b), is clearly predicated on the condition stated before, "If you abide in me, and my words abide in you" (v. 7a). To pray in Jesus' "name" (16:23) means to pray in a way that is consistent with Jesus' own character and purpose. Only those who learn and live Jesus' word can pray in this way.

Third and finally, the believer abides in Jesus and Jesus in the believer through *obedience* (15:9-17). As Jesus' love for the Father is demonstrated in his obedience, so the believer shows love for Jesus by doing the things Jesus asks (vv. 9-10; Luke 6:46). The disciples' highest duty is to "love one another" as they have been loved by Jesus (vv. 12, 17). Such devoted, sacrificial love will become a sign to the world of Jesus' divine authority and Sonship (17:21-23).

In my study, I keep a portrait of Jesus from my childhood. It is a picture of Jesus knocking at the door of a stone hamlet, surrounded by a garden. Called *Christ Knocking at Heart's Door* by artist Warner Sallman, the painting is a meditation on Revelation 3:20: "Behold, I stand at the door and knock. If anyone hears my voice and opens the door, I will come in and dine with him or her and he or she with me."

Whenever the pressures of my life and work start to build, I take a moment to gaze upon that image. It reminds me that the risen Lord is ready and willing, eager even, to enter and "abide" in me and for me to abide in him. But first, I must open the door and invite him in.

When I do, he brings his peace (14:27; 16:33; 20:21-22), his calm (14:1), and his joy (15:11; 16:20-22, 24; 17:13), and I am steadied by the assurance that Christ is in me and I am in Christ. Because of him, there is nothing to fear.

Yes, believers in every place and time face trouble (16:33a). But "be of good cheer," Jesus exclaims in triumph. "I have overcome the world!" (16:33b).

1. Think of a period in your life when you were deeply "troubled," yet also experienced a surprising peace. What helped you find God's calm at the center of the storm?

____

____

____

____

____

2. Using an online resource such as www.biblos.com, compare various English translations of "the Paraclete" in John 14:26. Which translation do you like best? What other words or images come to mind for this "Holy Friend" who "comes alongside to help"?

____

____

____

____

____

3. Do you agree that it was to the *advantage* of Jesus' disciples that he go away (16:17)? What "advantages" might we who know Jesus in the Spirit have over his first followers?

____

____

____

____

____

4. Drawing from John's five passages about the work of the Paraclete, write a job description for the Paraclete: (1) 14:16-17; (2) 14:25-26; (3) 15:26-27; (4) 16:7-11; and (5) 16:12-15.

5. Compare the personal dimension of the Paraclete's work in John 14–16 with the images of wind and breath for the Spirit in John 3:5-8 and water in John 4:14 and 7:38-39. Is the Holy Spirit more a "Person" or a "Power"?

6. How might Jesus' promise that the Spirit will bring new light to bear on Jesus' word (16:12-15) reassure and help the church in facing difficult issues? How has this principle helped the church in wrestling with issues like slavery and women's rights?

7. Why are organic metaphors like the vine and the branches so suggestive of spiritual growth? How is spiritual growth more like the growth of a plant than the operation of a microprocessor?

8. What insights from your knowledge of gardening might illumine God's "pruning" of the believer's life (15:2-3, 6)?

____

____

____

____

____

9. What disciplines of Scripture study, prayer, and service help you "abide" in Jesus?

____

____

____

____

____

The Paraclete's Sayings in John's Gospel

In the New Revised Standard translation, the "Paraclete" is rendered the "Advocate."

John 14:16-17
"And I will ask the Father, and he will give you another *Advocate*, to be with you forever. This is the Spirit of truth, whom the world cannot receive, because it neither sees him nor knows him. You know him, because he abides with you, and he will be in you."

John 14:25-26
"I have said these things to you while I am still with you. But the *Advocate,* the Holy Spirit, whom the Father will send in my name, will teach you everything, and remind you of all that I have said to you."

John 15:26-27
"When the *Advocate* comes, whom I will send to you from the Father, the Spirit of truth who comes from the Father, he will testify on my behalf. You also are to testify because you have been with me from the beginning."

John 16:7-11

"Nevertheless I tell you the truth: it is to your advantage that I go away, for if I do not go away, the *Advocate* will not come to you; but if I go, I will send him to you. And when he comes, he will prove the world wrong about sin and righteousness and judgment: about sin, because they do not believe in me; about righteousness, because I am going to the Father and you will see me no longer; about judgment, because the ruler of this world has been condemned."

John 16:12-15

"I still have many things to say to you, but you cannot bear them now. When the Spirit of truth comes, he will guide you into all the truth; for he will not speak on his own, but will speak whatever he hears, and he will declare to you the things that are to come. He will glorify me, because he will take what is mine and declare it to you. All that the Father has is mine. For this reason I said that he will take what is mine and declare it to you."

Session 10

Glorified; Lamb of God

John 12:20-36; 19:13-30

Recently, in a middle Georgia prison, a remarkable story of reconciliation and healing unfolded.

The story begins with a brother and sister whose mother was killed in a robbery gone awry. As a result of that tragedy, the family lost another brother and sister to suicide and committed a third sister to a mental institution. In time, the remaining brother and sister each divorced and developed debilitating health problems. No one can accuse these two of being sentimental about the cost of crime.

But in time, this brother and sister realized their thirst for vengeance was killing them. Out of self-preservation as well as Christian conviction, they found it within themselves to forgive their mother's killer.

This convict had spent most of his life behind bars, from age sixteen to the age of forty-something. Yet this brother and sister not only forgave him, but vowed to help him start his life over again. Standing before a room full of lifers, they embraced the man who took their mother from them.

Dr. Margaret H. Eskew, a member of the First Baptist Church of Christ, Macon, and associate professor of English in the College of Continuing and Professional Studies at Mercer University, was present when this happened. Since she had helped bring about the reconciliation, Margaret was asked to make a few remarks. She moved forward, searching for words to describe the miracle everyone had just witnessed. Here I'll let her take up the tale:

> Shocked because I had not prepared anything in advance, I walked toward the microphone having no idea what I could say. I looked out at that mass of men, most of whom were in prison

> for murder, and claimed with them the witness to the miracle of redemption, forgiveness, and grace, which was ours if we would arise and go to Jesus, for he would embrace us in his arms.

Margaret concluded by quoting the refrain of the hymn, "Come Ye Sinners, Poor and Needy": "In the arms of our dear Savior, O there are ten thousand charms."

After witnessing a miracle of forgiveness and then hearing Dr. Eskew's testimony, about sixty hardened criminals lined up to speak with her. In pain and longing, they asked one by one to know more about Jesus and his "ten thousand charms."

Those who find the notion of criminals being drawn to Jesus offensive or scandalous, please take it up with him. It was he who promised, "And when I am lifted up, I will draw *all people* to myself" (12:33).

The Hour Has Come (12:20-27)

Jesus' promise sounds in the story of Greek God-fearers seeking an audience with Jesus (vv. 21-22). After seeing Jesus welcomed to the Passover festival by adoring crowds (12:12-16) and hearing the buzz about his raising of Lazarus (12:9-11, 17-19), these visitors from afar want to meet the new religious superstar.

The Greek visitors seek Jesus' disciple, Philip, perhaps because "Philip" was a Greek name and he hailed from Galilee, where many Greek-speaking people lived: "Sir, we wish to see Jesus" (v. 21). Philip is uncertain about this request; until now, Jesus' ministry has largely been confined to the Jewish people (John 8:31; 12:11; 13:33; 19:19; Matt 15:24). Philip seeks advice from Andrew, another Galilean with a Greek name, who counsels that they take the matter to Jesus. When Philip and Andrew tell Jesus of the Greek's request to see him, Jesus nods gravely and answers, "The *hour has come* for the Son of Man to be glorified" (v. 23).

Such references to "the hour" are charged with meaning in John's Gospel. They push the action forward toward a momentous event yet to be. As early as the wedding in Cana, Jesus tells his mother "his hour has not come" (2:4). When Jesus' enemies try to arrest him, they cannot because "his hour had not come" (7:30; 8:20). In Jesus' encounter with the Greeks, we learn that the climatic "hour" is Jesus' death upon the cross (12:23-24, 27, 32-33).

Glorified (12:28-36)

Thus, with the appearance of the Greeks seeking Jesus, "the hour" has come for Jesus to be "glorified" (v. 23). "Glory" is a word heard often in John's Gospel. This Gospel begins with the dramatic declaration that God's glory—God's eternal essence, nature, and power—is decisively revealed in Jesus Christ: "And the Word became flesh and lived among us, and we have seen his *glory*, the *glory* as of a father's only son" (1:14).

Then at certain strategic moments in Jesus' ministry, this glory is revealed in striking ways. At the wedding in Cana, the first of Jesus' seven signs, the disciples see God's glory revealed when Jesus turns the water into wine (2:11). The raising of Lazarus in ch. 11 is prefaced by Jesus' promise that the Son of God will be *glorified* through the remarkable events about to unfold (11:4, 40).

But at the cross, God's costly, gracious, forgiving love shines forth in a way such love could never be revealed in Jesus' life alone. Like a seed that disappears into the earth and "dies," so Jesus' life must ebb away on the cross before the full power of his life and witness can be unleashed (12:24). Ironically, if these Greek pilgrims—and the larger world they represent (12:19)—are to "see" Jesus, then the radiance of God's glory and grace in Jesus must shine from his cross.

As the real flesh-and-blood person he is, Jesus cringes before the humiliation, suffering, and death that await him: "Now my soul is troubled. And what should I say—Father, save me from this hour?" (v. 27). Yet as the eternal Son of God, Jesus realizes "it is for this reason that I have come to this hour. Father, *glorify* your name" (v. 28).

The heavenly Father reassures Jesus in his moment of anguish: "I have glorified [my name], and I will glorify it again" (v. 28). The look backward—"I *have* glorified"—affirms Jesus' life and ministry coming to a close; the look forward—"I *will* glorify"—anticipates the fullest revelation of God's glory in Jesus' death and resurrection (7:39; 12:16; 13:1, 31-32; 16:25; 17:1, 4-5; 20:17).

In his wonderful little volume, *The Word Became Flesh*, E. Stanley Jones recalls the detonation of the first atomic bomb (New York: Abingdon, 1963). Seeing the blinding flash of light, physicist J. Robert Oppenheimer remarked that it reminded him of a passage from the *Bhagavad Gita*: "If the radiance of a thousand suns were burst into the sky, that would be like the splendor of the Mighty

One" (381). Such is the picture most people imagine when contemplating the glory of God.

But the radical, world-altering good news of Jesus is not first and foremost the glory of God's awe-inspiring power, but the glory of God's sacrificial, self-giving love. The glory of God in Jesus is not a blinding light that *sears* but a heartrending grace that *saves.*

The Son's eternal glory, shared with God the Father throughout eternity (17:5, 24), is about to be revealed in a shocking, scandalous, and infinitely costly way. Jesus will die as the final sign and seal of a divine love that will stop at nothing to find and reclaim God's lost, bewildered children (11:51-52).

Now Is the Judgment (12:31)

How then does Jesus' death so powerfully multiply the impact of his life? First by offering a devastating *judgment* on the world's sin and evil: "Now is the *judgment* of this world," says Jesus. "Now the ruler of this world will be driven out" (v. 33).

The story of Jesus' betrayal and arrest (18:1-11), grilling before the religious authorities (18:12-13, 19-24), and trial before the Roman governor, Pilate (18:28–19:16) presents a disturbing exposé of justice run amuck. Jesus' enemies are intent on destroying him and silencing his truth; Pilate is interested in keeping the peace and preserving his privileged position (18:38; 19:12-13). As a result, the "world" as represented by religion and government is judged as so "blind" to God's truth that it crucifies the very Son of God (3:19-20)!

But the cross is not just a devastating judgment of the sin of the *world*; the cross is a devastating judgment of *my* sin, *my* petty lies and convenient compromises, *my* proud insistence on going *my* way instead of God's way. I still remember when the Holy Spirit turned the searchlight of God's truth on my life. To be sure, as a boy of nine, I was no great sinner as the world measures such things. But it was a terrible day when I realized in my heart of hearts that Jesus didn't just die for the world. Jesus died for *me*!

In John's Gospel, Jesus always takes pains to confront people with the truth of *their* need for God's forgiveness and saving grace. This is evident in his encounters with Nicodemus (3:3-10), the woman at the well (4:16-18), the woman caught in adultery (8:10-11), and Simon Peter (21:15-17). Still today, the Holy Spirit convicts persons of their own guilt and need for forgiveness (16:8-11). As Canon Peter Green has written, "Only the [one] who . . . owns his [or her] share in the guilt of the cross, may claim his [or her] share in its grace" (in John R. W. Stott, *The Cross of Christ* [Downers Grove IL: Inter-Varsity Press, 1986] 60).

"And When I Am Lifted Up" (12:32)

Thank God, the cross is not only a judgment. If it were, the cross would only have the power to condemn. Yet "God did not send the Son into the world to condemn the world, but in order that the world might be saved through him" (3:17). This is the great paradox at the heart of the gospel: on the one hand, Jesus' cross brings the most devastating of judgments (12:31), but on the other, Jesus' cross shatters that judgment with a shocking, unspeakable grace: "And when I am *lifted up* from the earth, I will draw all people to myself" (12:32).

Jesus' use of the phrase "lifted up" is deeply ironic. It is as Jesus is "lifted up" on his cross that he—like the bronze serpent Moses raised above the children of Israel in the wilderness—will bring forgiveness, healing, and new life to those who trust in him (3:14-15; Num 21:9-10).

The Lamb of God (19:13-30)

The reckless, extravagant love for the world finds its fullest expression in Jesus' death upon the cross (3:16). There Jesus reveals himself to be the "the Lamb of God who takes away the sin of the world" (1:29, 36). This poignant title recalls the Passover lamb sacrificed by each Hebrew household during the tenth plague in Egypt (Exod 12:1-13). The faithful were to smear some of the lamb's blood on their doorpost so the avenging angel would "pass over" their homes, hence, the festival's name, "Passover" (v. 13).

John's Gospel is careful to note that Jesus was crucified on "the day of *Preparation* for the Passover" (19:14, italics mine) at "about noon," the very hour when the slaughtering of the Passover lambs began (v. 14).

Yet while Jesus is the Passover Lamb, this passive image must be balanced by the recognition that he is also the Good Shepherd who *willingly* lays down his life for the sheep (10:11). Jesus is both priest *and* sacrifice (Heb 9:11-14; 10:10-14). He is no hapless pawn in events that spiral out of control: "No one takes my life from me," he boldly proclaims. "I *lay* it down" (John 10:18). Yet if dying an unjust death on a criminal's cross is what it takes to reveal once and for all God's inexhaustible, unconditional love, Jesus is willing to make the ultimate sacrifice: "No one has greater love than this, to lay down one's life for one's friends" (15:13; Heb 9:26).

Chuck Colson, founder of Prison Fellowship, visited a prison in Brazil that was based on Christian principles. In this well-run prison, the inmates were kind and considerate. Bible verses were written on every wall.

An inmate led Colson to view solitary confinement. When the massive door was opened, Colson saw hanging from the far wall an ornate, beautifully carved crucifix of Jesus on his cross. Head down, eyes lowered, the prisoner at Colson's elbow whispered, "He's doing time for the rest of us."

Most believers intuitively know—even if they cannot fully fathom how or why—that Jesus' death as the Lamb of God took the punishment deserved by a fallen world, discharging it in Jesus' own suffering (Isa 53:4-6; 2 Cor 5:21; 1 Pet 3:18).

This should not be construed to mean Jesus "paid off" an angry, vengeful God, as the cross is tragically misunderstood in some Christian circles. Instead, the cross means Jesus—and the loving heavenly Father he brought near—made the ultimate sacrifice in pressing home the truth of God's unconditional love.

Rather than answer the world's ridicule and rejection, scorn and shame, torture and crucifixion of the Son with an avenging wrath, God answered with a costly, gracious, forgiving love. In a mystery beyond telling, out of God's broken heart poured the salvation of the world (John 1:29, 36; 1 John 2:2; Rom 5:8; 2 Cor 5:19).

"It Is Finished" (19:30)

Jesus' last words, uttered from his cross, are "It is finished" (19:30).

Yes, Jesus' suffering and death are finally done. But even more important, Jesus has "finished the work" the Father gave him to do (17:4; 4:34; 5:36), namely, the work of revealing God's eternal grace and glory. The height of that glory and the depth of that grace are revealed most fully at Jesus' cross. There the defiant light of God's costly, forgiving love shines in the darkness of the world's sin and evil, and *no* darkness—not even the crushing darkness that gathers around the cross—can put it out (1:5).

God has done all God can do. Now each of us must decide if we will accept the "indescribable gift" of God's gracious forgiveness, love, and new life in Jesus Christ (2 Cor 9:15). For as Jesus is "lifted up" on his cross, the scandalous yet liberating invitation sounds,

Come, ye sinners, poor and needy,
Weak and wounded, sick and sore;
Jesus ready stands to save you,
Full of pity, love and pow'r.

I will arise and go to Jesus,
He will embrace me in His arms;
In the arms of my dear Savior,
Oh, there are ten thousand charms.

Can you hear the music?

1. The Apostle Paul calls the cross a "stumbling block to Jews and foolishness to Gentiles" (1 Cor 1:23). By contrast, John's Gospel emphasizes the magnetic power of the cross: "I will draw all people to myself" (12:33). Can the cross be both?

____

____

____

____

____

2. Did Jesus have to die on the cross to save the world from sin? Why does the logic of John's argument require a "yes" answer to that question (3:19-20; 12:33)? Why is Jesus the "Lamb slain *from the foundation of the world*" (Rev 13:8, italics mine)?

____

____

____

____

____

3. Are you disturbed by the notion of Jesus as the "Lamb of God" sacrificed for your sins? Saddened? Convicted? Comforted?

4. Name some of history's most famous martyrs. How is Jesus' sacrificial death *similar to* that of other martyrs who died unjustly for a noble cause? How is Jesus' death *different*?

5. What are your favorite hymns, spirituals, or other songs about the cross? What touches you most deeply?

6. Do you have a favorite painting, stained-glass window, sculpture, or other depiction of the crucifixion? What moves you about this particular portrayal of Christ's death?

7. Do you wear a cross in some form? If so, what does wearing that cross mean to you?

____

____

____

____

____

8. If being forgiven and spiritually reborn is a gift (John 3:16; 2 Cor 9:15), how is that gift received? John 1:10-13; Mark 1:14-15; 8:34; and Acts 2:37-39 may help you formulate an answer.

____

____

____

____

____

9. In what way is the following equation true for you: "1 Cross + 3 Nails = 4Given"? How would you express the meaning of Christ's death upon the cross in your own words?

____

____

____

____

____

Session 11

Blessed

John 20:1-31

In the years before radio or television, people often recited poetry as a form of entertainment. On one such occasion, an English hostess asked a renowned actor to recite the 23rd Psalm. He did so with all the polish and flourish worthy of his profession. Those present rewarded him with polite applause.

Another gentleman in attendance was known to be a man of deep devotion. Several asked that he also recite that most beloved of psalms. After resisting, he finally agreed.

When this man spoke, the perfect elocution and mastery of the first speaker was gone, but in its place was the quiet conviction of one intimately acquainted with the living God. The audience was moved. This time there was no applause, just quiet, reverent appreciation.

In the silence that followed, everyone wondered why the second speaker's testimony rang so fresh and true. Being a consummate professional, the actor knew the answer. "I only know the psalm," he explained. "*He* knows the *Shepherd*."

There is a world of difference in knowing *about* Jesus and knowing *him* (Phil 3:10a)!

John's Gospel was written to answer the question, "How can people believe in something, in *Someone*, they have never seen?" (20:29, 30-31). Granted, today's generations of believers have not seen Jesus either in the flesh or in the radiance of his Easter glory. We must rely on the testimony of his first disciples to learn about him (John 20:30-31; 21:24-25; 1 John 1:1-3; 2 Pet 1:16-18).

But believers in every age have known the mystery of Christ's unseen but sometimes deeply felt presence in ways that are consistent with the New Testament witness. In the immortal words of the great Scottish divine, George MacDonald, "We are haunted by the scent of unseen roses." Or as the Gospel of John sounds the precious promise, "Blessed are those who have not seen and yet have come to believe" (20:29).

The Empty Tomb (20:1-13)

All four Gospels report that early on the Sunday morning following Jesus' death, some women discovered Jesus' tomb was empty. John's Gospel focuses on Mary Magdalene, though other women are implied in the "we" of v. 2. Mary Magdalene comes to the tomb while "it is still dark" (v. 1), consistent with this Gospel's emphasis on night and darkness as symbolic of unbelief.

Mary is shocked to see the stone rolled away (v. 1), but the empty tomb doesn't lead her to believe Jesus is risen. To the contrary, she assumes someone has desecrated or otherwise disturbed Jesus' resting place. Mary runs for help, breathlessly telling Peter and the Beloved Disciple, "They have taken the Lord out of the tomb, and we do not know where they have laid him!" (v. 2).

Peter and the Beloved Disciple race to the tomb and find the burial wrappings of Jesus (v. 5). Upon closer examination, they discover that the linen burial cloths of Jesus are neatly stacked in two piles, the turban head roll and the body wrap just below it (vv. 6-7). Clearly, this is not the work of grave robbers. Grave robbers don't strip a corpse and then neatly stack the burial wrappings like a meticulous maid. Rather, as the Beloved Disciple—the superstar of faith in John's Gospel—is first to see, those folded grave clothes mean Jesus has vanquished sin and death (v. 8b).

After Peter and the Beloved Disciple "return to their homes" (v. 10), Mary lingers, weeping outside the empty tomb (v. 11). Through her tears, she peers inside and sees two angels, one sitting where the head and the other where the body of Jesus had rested (vv. 11-12).

Once while teaching a Bible study, I asked those gathered why John's Gospel puts such emphasis on the grave clothes and the placement of the angels. One gentleman—a detective—observed that at the scene of a murder, the officers start by tagging the feet of the victim. But if the officers come upon a crime scene where the victim is still alive, they start at the head. A rescuer cradles the victim's head because that's where life is and where life-saving measures are administered.

"There weren't two angels at Jesus' feet," my detective friend suggested, "because Jesus was no longer dead. No, one angel was working at his head, unwrapping his bandages, welcoming him back to life!"

Regardless of whether that intriguing insight is correct, this much is certain: the pained attention to detail about the empty tomb and the grave clothes is meant to leave us thunderstruck at the news of Jesus' resurrection. The resurrection John's Gospel proclaims is not poetic language for the great hope of life beyond the grave. The ancient world was already full of stories and language like that (see N. T. Wright, *Surprised by Hope* [New York: HarperOne, 2008] 35–51). No, resurrection means Jesus literally and bodily vacated his tomb in a new, concrete, and tangible expression of his person, a sign forevermore of God's power to restore and recreate a fallen world (1 Cor 15:20-28).

Resurrection means God reversed the verdict of the corrupt religious and political establishment that crucified his Son (Acts 2:36; Rom 1:4). Resurrection means Jesus robbed death of its prey and emerged from the tomb radiant with the glory of a life and love that will never die (Rom 8:31-39). Resurrection means those lost to us are not lost to God but wait for us even now in the Father's house (John 14:1). Because Jesus lives, those who trust in him also live, now and forevermore (John 11:25-26).

Unlike Lazarus who stumbled from his tomb with the tendrils of his grave clothes yet clinging (John 11:44), Jesus' grave clothes are left behind like the crisp cocoon of a butterfly now soaring in glory. Unlike Lazarus, Jesus won't need his grave clothes again.

The Appearance to Mary in Her Grief (20:14-18)

Despite the crucial importance of the empty tomb, the empty tomb alone did not ignite an Easter faith; it took the appearances of the risen Lord to do that. The evidence of the empty tomb raised the question the appearances of the risen Lord emphatically answered: "He is not *here*" because "*He* is risen!" (Luke 24:5).

In quick succession, John sketches five scenes in which the risen Lord appears. Jesus appears to Mary in her *grief* (John 20:11-18), to the disciples in their *fear* (vv. 19-23), to Thomas in his *doubt* (vv. 24-29), to seven fishermen in their *hopelessness* (21:1-14), and to Peter in his *guilt* (21:15-19) (as suggested by Kevin Quast, *Reading the Gospel of John* [New York: Paulist Press, 1991] 130). In each case, the encounter is custom fitted to the needs of the persons involved. Mary Magdalene, for instance, is told *not* to cling to Jesus (20:17), while Thomas is invited to touch the wounds in the Master's hands and side (20:27). There is no one-size-fits-all faith, either then or now.

Mary's encounter with the risen Lord begins with the angels' question, "Woman, why are you weeping?" (v. 13a). The question suggests that tears are inappropriate since Jesus has risen from the dead.

But Mary, still blind to her Lord's triumph, erupts in anguish, "They have taken the Lord out of the tomb, and we do not know where they have laid him!" (v. 13b). She then turns around and sees Jesus, though Mary does not recognize him (v. 14).

Jesus asks the same question as the angels, "Why are you weeping?" and adds another, "Whom are you looking for?" (v. 15). Still trying to determine who moved Jesus' body, Mary wonders if the stranger standing before her might be the gardener (v. 15b); Jesus was buried in a garden, after all (19:41).

The probing questions asked by the angels and Jesus prove powerless to open Mary's eyes to the miracle standing before her. Only when Jesus lovingly calls her by name—"Mary!"—does she recognize him (20:16). Earlier in John's Gospel, Jesus the Good Shepherd declared he knew his sheep by name. When he calls their name, they recognize the Shepherd's voice and follow him (10:3-4). Now by the empty tomb, that promise proves true.

Thus, faith in the risen Christ is not simply a deduction drawn from the evidence. As Mary turns *from* the empty tomb (v. 14a), she is confronted *by* the risen Lord. But she can only "see" him when her eyes are "opened" to the stunning reality of his triumph over sin and death (1:51; 9:10, 30; Luke 24:31, 45). Jesus opens her eyes by calling her name.

The appearance of the risen Jesus by his empty tomb moves Mary from overwhelming despair to hope to faith to mission: "Go to my brothers and say to them, 'I am ascending to my Father and your Father, to my God and your God'" (v. 17).

An ecstatic Mary does as her Lord commands: she rushes to the other disciples, bearing the great, glad news of Easter: "I have seen the Lord!" (v. 18).

The Appearance to the Disciples in Their Fear (20:19-23)

In response to Mary's witness—and the report of Peter and the Beloved Disciple—the disciples gather that Sunday evening. But they meet behind locked doors, fearing Jesus' enemies will now come looking for them (v. 19). Neither the report of an empty tomb nor Mary's confession are sufficient to convince them Jesus is alive.

Suddenly, the risen Lord appears, slipping past locked doors like the sunrise peeking through curtains. Standing among the disciples, Jesus greets them with the customary Jewish greeting: "Peace be with you!" Then he shows the disciples the wounds on his hands and side.

Clearly, Jesus' resurrected body is not just a resuscitated corpse but a marvelously transformed expression of himself. Nor is the risen Jesus bound by the limits of time and space. He can appear and disappear at will, yet he is clearly recognizable as the disciples' beloved Master. His distinctive scars provide compelling proof of his identity: "The disciples were overjoyed when they saw the Lord!" (v. 20).

Once more, Jesus says, "Peace be with you!" (v. 21), but this time, it is clear this is no ordinary greeting. Jesus' wounds reveal the incalculable cost of making good on his earlier promise, "Peace I leave with you; my peace I give you. I do not give to you as the world gives. Do not let your hearts be troubled and do not be afraid" (14:27).

Then comes perhaps the most beautiful brush stroke in the story: Jesus *breathes* on his disciples and says, "Receive the Holy Spirit" (20:22). His gesture recalls God breathing into Adam's nostrils the breath of life (Gen 2:7). Once more, God is breathing life into God's beloved but fallen creatures, now reborn through the indwelling presence and power of God's own Spirit.

In this climatic act, the many promises about the Holy Spirit that animate John's Gospel find their fulfillment. The risen Lord *baptizes*—literally, "immerses"—in the Holy Spirit those who trust in him (1:32-33). The Spirit brings the new birth Jesus promised (3:5-8). The Spirit is the wellspring of the new life Jesus gives (4:13-14; 6:63; 7:37-39). The Spirit is the Paraclete, the one who brings Jesus near (14:18, 25-27). Thus, by breathing his own life, his own Spirit, into his disciples, Jesus gives the "peace that surpasses understanding" (Phil 4:7).

But for the disciples, as for Mary, the gift of Christ's risen presence and peace is not for them alone: it is a message, an offer, a hope for the world! As Mary was commissioned to proclaim the risen Lord's triumph, so are the disciples: "As the Father has sent me, I am sending you" (20:21; 17:18). In the proclamation of Jesus' life, death, and resurrection—and in the living out of that story in the life of the church—God's gift of forgiveness and new life is made to all who will receive it (20:23; 13:34; 15:12-13, 17; 1 John 3:23-24). Thus, in the gift of the Holy Spirit, the disciples are renewed and empowered for their mission to the world.

The Appearance to Thomas in His Doubt (20:24-29)

One disciple is missing that first Sunday night when Jesus makes his surprise appearance: Thomas (v. 24). With his story, the focus shifts from those who "have seen" to those who "have *not* seen, and yet believe" (vv. 29-31).

Thomas has been immortalized in Christian tradition as *Doubting* Thomas. From the glimpses we see of him in John's Gospel, he does appear to be an independent thinker (11:16; 14:5; 20:24). In fairness, though, Thomas does not ask for anything the other disciples have not received, namely, the chance to see the risen Lord for himself (v. 25).

Despite his doubts, Thomas longs to believe, so the next Sunday when the disciples gather, he is among them (v. 26). The drama from the week before is recreated as the resurrected Jesus slips past locked doors once again and brings his signal greeting, "Peace be with you" (v. 26). This time, Jesus adds an invitation uniquely crafted to Thomas's need: "Put your finger here and see my hands. Reach out your hand and put it in my side. Do not doubt but believe" (v. 27).

Gaping in wonder, Thomas responds with heartfelt awe: "My Lord and my God!" (v. 28). From the deepest doubt in John's Gospel springs the highest confession.

Blessed Are Those Who Have Not Seen and Yet Believe (20:30-31)

Thomas's experience—like that of Mary and the other disciples—is unique to his time and place. His faith in the risen Lord is awakened by what he *sees* (v. 29b). But Jesus' risen presence and the peace he brings can also be experienced by those who have *not seen and yet believe* (v. 29b).

In Michael Green's book *Who Is This Jesus?*, he notes that for years he believed Jesus was a great and noble man, but dead as the proverbial doornail. Then, like dawn creeping over the horizon, Green began to sense that the promise of Easter might actually be true. "And the most momentous consequence of all this?" he writes. "[Jesus] is still around! I still recall the force with which this struck me at the time I was beginning to become a disciple of his. If he rose, he must be alive. If he is alive, should I not meet him? And I did" (Nashville: Thomas Nelson Inc., 1992, p. 87).

The Gospel of John was written to call forth just such an encounter (20:31), and the confession of countless believers throughout the ages reveals how perfectly John's witness hit its mark: "Though you have not seen him, you love him; and even though you do not see him now, you believe in him and are filled with an inexpressible and glorious joy" (1 Pet 1:8, NIV).

1. Do you agree that an empty tomb signifying Jesus' *bodily* resurrection is essential to a vital Christian faith? Why does the New Testament argue that a belief in a "spiritualized" or metaphoric resurrection is not enough (see 1 Cor 15:3-8, 12-20)?

____

____

____

____

____

2. Why does Mary see two angels inside the empty tomb when Peter and the Beloved Disciple do not? Might her lingering and tears hint at an answer (vv. 11-15)?

____

____

____

____

____

3. In the experience of the believing community today, what does it mean for Jesus to "call your name" (20:16; 10:3-5)?

4. Mary Magdalene is the first witness to see the risen Lord and the first evangelist (vv. 17-18). Women also appear at strategic points elsewhere in John's Gospel (2:1-11; 4:1-42; 8:1-11; 11:20-44; 12:1-8; 19:25-27; 20:1-18). What does this suggest about the role of women in Jesus' life and ministry? In the church today?

5. Compare the depiction of Jesus' resurrected body in John 20 with Paul's exploration of the resurrected body in 1 Corinthians 15:35-57. In two columns titled "Physical Body" and "Resurrection Body," list the characteristics of each.

6. Why does Jesus emerge from his tomb still bearing the scars of his crucifixion? Why do Jesus' scars remain forever as a sign of his triumph (Rev 5:6, 9, 12; John 1:29, 36)?

7. What are some of the positive aspects of Thomas's doubt? What happens to a faith, a believer, or a church that permits no doubt?

8. Can you describe a time when you were surprised by the presence and peace of Jesus Christ in the face of a grief like Mary's? A fear like the disciples'? A doubt like Thomas's?

9. In Christian tradition, Easter is sometimes called the "Eighth Day of Creation," signifying the *re*-creation of the world. How does Jesus' resurrection recreate the world?

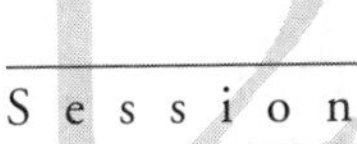

Session 12

Bread and Fish

John 21:1-17

Apart from the surprise of the risen Christ showing up to cook breakfast on the beach, the greatest surprise of John 21 is that this chapter is included at all. John's Gospel seems to end at the end of chapter 20: "Now Jesus did many other signs in the presence of his disciples, which are not written in this book. But these are written so that you may come to believe that Jesus is the Messiah, the Son of God, and that through believing you may have life in his name" (vv. 30-31).

But when one turns the page to chapter 21, it's as though the dramatic encounters with the risen Lord in the previous chapter never happened. Peter, Thomas, the Beloved Disciple, and four other disciples are suddenly sixty-five miles north of Jerusalem where we saw them last, back home in Galilee (vv. 1-3). They seem oblivious to Jesus' triumph over sin and death and his living Presence at work in the world. Further, the mission the risen Lord gave his disciples in John 20:21-23 seems to have been ditched for a return to the fishing trade (21:3). In fact, the disconnect between John 20 and 21 is so great that many scholars believe chapter 21 was added later as an appendix or epilogue to the Gospel.

While that may be true, the recognition that chapter 21 was added by a later hand doesn't greatly alter our approach to the text. Whoever put this Gospel into its final form was certainly aware of the abruptness of the transition between the two chapters. Still, the final editors of John's Gospel left the sharp break between chapter 20 and 21 in place because it made theological sense to them, as it does to me.

Why, for example, is the Sunday after Easter one of the most poorly attended of the year? Just one week before, everyone was present, joyfully singing "Christ the Lord Is Risen Today!" but one week later, more seats than usual are empty. As judged by worship participation, it's as though Easter never happened. Maybe the apparent contradiction between John 20 and John 21 is not so great as it appears!

In the liturgy of the church, the Sunday after Easter is called "Low Sunday," a term that points to the stark contrast between Easter Sunday and the Sunday after. John 20 is about Easter Sunday. John 21 is about the Sunday *after* Easter and all the other Sundays, Mondays, and other days the church forgets Jesus truly is let loose in the world, waiting to surprise us with his glory and grace.

Breakfast with Jesus (21:1-8)

John 21 opens on a dismal note: Peter and six of his fellow disciples spend a long, fruitless night fishing. They greet the dawn weary and hungry with not a single fish to cook for breakfast (v. 3b).

"Boys, you haven't caught any fish, have you?" shouts a stranger from shore (v. 5). A hundred yards out (v. 8b), the disciples turn to see who so pointedly names their failure. No one realizes it is Jesus (v. 4b). "Cast your net on the other side," he tells them, "and I bet you'll catch some" (v. 6).

Perhaps expecting to prove the stranger wrong, the disciples do as suggested. Yet the catch is immediate and so huge that they cannot hoist the bulging net into the boat (v. 6). That's when the Beloved Disciple takes a second look at the figure shrouded in the morning mist. "It is the Lord!" he cries (v. 7). Everyone turns to look and sees it is indeed Jesus, radiant with Easter light. Seeing the Master's broad, toothy grin, Peter dives in and eagerly swims to shore. The others follow in the boat, dragging the full net behind them (v. 8).

Once on shore, the disciples find the risen Jesus cooking breakfast over a bed of hot coals. The fire knocks back the morning chill, and the aroma of sizzling fish and baked bread wafts through the air (v. 9). Just as everyone is settling down to dine, Jesus tells his disciples, "Go bring some of the fish you just caught" (v. 10).

It seems a strange request since Jesus is already cooking fish when the disciples arrive. Surely, the Lord who turned five loaves and two fish into a feast for five thousand (6:1-14) doesn't "need" any fish from the disciples! Why ask for some?

Maybe because Jesus wants the disciples to connect their failed fishing expedition with his warning earlier in John's Gospel, "Apart from me you can do *nothing!*" (15:5b). Maybe he wants to press home the realization that all those fish were caught at *his* command. Or maybe Jesus wants his disciples to remember the mission they have forsaken, fishing for *people* (Matt 4:19; Mark 1:17; Luke 5:10)!

Years ago, one of my predecessors at the First Baptist Church of Christ in Macon, Dr. Albert Cardwell, stopped by a men's prayer breakfast at the church. Dr. Cardwell was known for his stout, bull-dog build and gruff, no-nonsense matter.

"What are you doing here?" Dr. Cardwell asked the men gathered in the church's fellowship hall.

"Well, Preacher, we're having breakfast," someone answered.

"I can see that," said Dr. Cardwell. "But what are you *doing* here?"

Looking a bit bewildered, the spokesman responded, "Like I said, we're having breakfast."

"I know you're having breakfast," Dr. Cardwell replied, "but what are you *doing* here?" Then he turned on his heels and left, leaving the prayer breakfast crowd gaping after him.

As Jesus sends his disciples back to the boat to fetch some more fish, that is the unspoken question he means to sound in their minds and hearts: "What are you *doing* here, taking your ease in Galilee, when I commissioned you to take the good news of my love to all the world?" (3:16; 17:18; 20:21-23).

Fish and Bread (6:1-14)

Earlier in John's Gospel, Jesus feeds his disciples and a crowd of five thousand (6:10) loaves and fish. That story also starts with want (6:9) and ends in plenty (6:12-13) because Christ is present in purpose and power.

But now, the second time Jesus serves his disciples loaves and fish, there are not two fish (6:9) but 153 (21:11)! In this highly symbolic Gospel, the number 153 likely carries within it some deeper spiritual meaning. The problem is that we have lost the key!

Through the centuries, there has been no lack of inventive explanations as to the significance of the number 153. Perhaps the most convincing is Jerome's fourth-century observation that there were 153 kinds of fish in the sea. Thus, this catch encompassing every kind of fish symbolizes the church's mission to every tribe and nation. Whatever the exact symbolism of the number 153, the general meaning seems clear: the surprisingly large catch signifies the universal scope and reach of the church's mission.

Besides fish, there is another item on the breakfast menu that morning when Jesus pulls out his skillet by the sea: bread. Bread is even richer in biblical associations than fish! It was manna, the "bread of heaven," that sustained the children of Israel in the wilderness (Exod 16:4). Jesus taught his disciples to pray, "Give us this day our daily bread" (Matt 6:11). As already noted, earlier in John's Gospel, Jesus feeds his disciples and a teeming multitude fish and bread. That story begins with the question, "Where are we to buy *bread* for these people to eat?" (6:5). At the Last Supper, Jesus takes a loaf of bread, breaks and blesses it, and gives it to his disciples, saying, "Take, eat, this is my body" (Matt 26:26; Mark 14:22; Luke 22:19).

That riveting morning on the beach, Jesus provides a home-cooked breakfast for his disciples, prepared with his own loving hands. But Jesus did not come merely to meet physical needs, but to awaken abundant life, eternal life, life in him that starts now and lasts forever (John 3:36; 10:10, 28).

Jesus admonishes the crowd following the multiplication of the loaves and fish in John 6: "Very truly, I tell you, you are looking for me, not because you saw signs, but because you ate your fill of the loaves. Do not work for the food that perishes, but for the food that endures for eternal life, which the Son of Man will give you" (vv. 26-27). Now on the far side of Easter, standing in the presence of the one who gave his life for them and for the world, the disciples realize in the profoundest possible way why Jesus is indeed the "bread of *life*!" (6:35, 48).

In an episode of the classic television series *M*A*S*H*, Major Winchester's protective shell finally cracks before the horrors of war. He slips into a deep depression, searching for answers but finding none. Eventually, he wanders from the base hospital to the battalion aid station where the wounded are first taken. The major stands there trance-like, surveying the carnage, when a medical corpsman calls him to the side of a dying soldier. Stone-faced, with no touch of feeling, Winchester confirms the impending death.

But then the mortally wounded soldier cries out, "I can't see anything! Hold my hand!" Feeling awkward and inept, the major does. "I'm dying," moans the soldier.

The soldier's wrenching words awaken the questions tugging at the major's troubled heart. His own fears and misgivings come pouring out: "Can you see anything?" he asks. "Can you feel anything? I have to know!"

For a long moment, there is no answer. Then a look of calm settles over the soldier's face as, just before he dies, he whispers, "I smell bread."

There is no missing the meaning: freshly baked bread is the smell of hope. Freshly baked bread is the sign of Christ's unseen but sustaining presence.

Jesus and Peter: "Do You Love Me?" (21:9-14)

What began as a failed fishing expedition ends in abundance and plenty because Jesus comes to his defeated, despondent disciples "in this way" (21:1). The risen Lord is "made known" to his disciples "in the breaking of the bread" (Luke 24:35; Acts 2:42, 46), a miracle reenacted in some measure every time the church gathers before the Lord's Table. Thus, at a surprise breakfast on the beach, the disciples are restored to spiritual vitality and life in the presence of the Master. What a glorious ending to a story that began on a sad and somber note!

Only this is not the end of the story. There is yet another movement, and a painful one at that, in which the church's life and mission come even more clearly into focus. As the disciples take their ease by the sea, their stomachs and hearts full, Jesus shatters the picture-perfect moment with a question that sounds with the shrillness of a pitch-cracking crystal. Perhaps indicating the other disciples with a sweep of his hand, he asks, "Simon, son of John, do you love me more than these?" (v. 15).

Peter drops his eyes as his fellow disciples look away in embarrassment. The question recalls Peter's brash promise the night of Jesus' betrayal: "Though all the rest desert you, I'll stand by you till the end!" (Matt 26:33; Mark 14:29; Luke 22:33; John 13:37).

Head bowed, the strapping fisherman answers softly, "Yes, Lord, you know that I love you."

"Then feed my lambs," says Jesus, "feed my lambs."

There is an awkward silence, and then everyone breathes a collective sigh of relief. Now the party can get back on track. Only Jesus isn't done. A second time he asks Peter, "Simon, son of John, do you love me?" (v. 16).

The disciples shoot one another quizzical looks. Why is Jesus twisting the dagger? Why not let bygones be bygones?

Peter answers with trembling lips, "Yes, Lord, you know that I love you."

Jesus answers, "Then tend my sheep" (v. 16).

Yet once more, Jesus asks the probing question: "Simon, son of John, do you love me?" (v. 17).

This time, Peter is deeply wounded. His broad shoulders shake as painful memories flood his soul (v. 17b).

With Jesus' question hanging in the air, Peter lifts his head and brushes back the tears. He looks searchingly, defiantly into Jesus' eyes: "Lord, you know everything. You *know* that I love you!" (v. 17c).

Jesus holds Peter's gaze. No hurt in Jesus and no shame in Peter can break that gaze. Finally, Jesus nods and says, "Then feed my sheep. And come what may, 'Follow me'" (see vv. 17-19).

"Do you love me?" Why does Jesus ask—and why must Peter answer—the painful question not once but three times? The answer lies in the "charcoal fire" Jesus prepares on the beach (v. 9). The Greek word for "charcoal fire" is found only twice in the New Testament, here and in John 18:18. As Peter warms himself over just such a fire outside the high priest's house, he denies his Lord *three* times (18:15-18, 25-27).

In preparing a charcoal fire on the beach, Jesus recreates the moment of Peter's greatest failure and betrayal. So now, on the far side of his cross and resurrection, Jesus asks the pointed question, "Do you love me?" not once, but three times, because the poison of each of Peter's betrayals must be vanquished by the healing power of Jesus' love.

Feed My Sheep

In a painful but liberating encounter with the risen Lord, Peter is restored to service. He and his fellow disciples have a job to do, namely, to "feed the *lambs*"—perhaps signifying new believers (v. 15)—and "tend and feed the *sheep*"—perhaps suggesting the more mature members of the church (vv. 16-17).

Thus, John 21 provides a fitting climax to John's Gospel. In the power of Jesus' risen life, the disciples are to cast and gather the net of the Christian witness (21:5-6, 10-11). They must proclaim and embody the good news of God's forgiveness (20:23). And they must feed and tend the flock of those who listen for the voice of the Good Shepherd (10:3-4) and manifest in their loving fellowship the radical, accepting grace he alone makes possible (John 13:34; 15:12; 17:21; 2 John 1:5).

General Mills proclaims its Wheaties cereal the "Breakfast of Champions." While that may be true for athletes, for Christians, the "breakfast of champions" is bread and fish: bread signifying the presence of the risen Christ and fish signifying the mission to which all believers are called.

Yes, in a surprise breakfast on the beach, Jesus gives hope to his church and to the world. For in the power of his risen life, we can at last be who we need to be and do what we need to do.

1. What is breakfast like at your house? Do you ever enjoy a full breakfast, rich in food and fellowship, like the one Jesus shared with his disciples on the beach? Have you ever eaten breakfast on the beach?

____

____

____

____

____

2. Compare the stories of bread and fish in John 21:1-14 and John 6:1-71. How does the disciples' breakfast with the risen Lord on the beach fill out their understanding of Jesus as "the bread of life"?

____

____

____

____

____

3. When taking the Lord's Supper, do you feel a special intimacy with Jesus? Can you remember a Lord's Supper service that was especially meaningful for you? What made it so?

____

____

____

____

____

4. Besides the Lord's Supper, what are some other ways Jesus is made known in the "breaking of the bread"? For help, see Luke 24:35; Acts 2:42, 46; 20:7, 11.

5. Why does real forgiveness often require the sort of painful confrontation Jesus evokes with Peter?

6. Why is Peter's confession, "Lord, you know everything; you know that I love you" (v. 17) much more promising than his earlier pledge to stand by Jesus till the end (13:37)?

7. If Jesus asked, "Do you love me?" what would you say? What might you say the second time he asked? The third?

8. Which of the facets of the church's mission, "catching the fish" or "feeding the sheep," comes more naturally to you or your congregation? What happens when a church does one but not the other?

9. Which part of the story in John 21:1-17 touches you most deeply? Where do you most ache for Jesus' hopeful, healing presence? Where do you most need to hear and heed his challenge?

Epilogue

You Are the Beloved Disciple!

John 21:20-25

After soaring to lofty heights of revelation and glory and plumbing the depths of a stunning, sacrificial love, the Gospel of John closes on a seemingly mundane note: Peter worrying about whom Jesus loves best, *him* or the Beloved Disciple!

It appears Peter has eyed the Beloved Disciple for a long time. Peter knows the Beloved Disciple rested his head on Jesus' chest at the Last Supper (21:20b; 13:23-26). Peter knows Jesus entrusted the care of his mother to the Beloved Disciple (19:26-27). Peter remembers racing the Beloved Disciple to the empty tomb and losing the contest (20:4); and the Beloved Disciple not only *outran* him but out-*believed* him (20:8; 21:7)! For all these reasons and more, Peter fears that the Beloved Disciple is Jesus' favorite, a title he covets for himself.

Thus, when Jesus tells Peter to "follow me" (21:19) after their painful encounter on the beach, Peter takes only a few steps before turning to check out the competition (v. 20). Nodding at the Beloved Disciple, trailing behind, he asks Jesus, "What about him?" (v. 22).

Jesus bristles at Peter's question (v. 22). What the future holds for the Beloved Disciple is not Peter's concern. Peter has only one job to do, one consuming passion to propel him through life, and that is to follow Jesus! It is only as Peter follows Jesus—and grows a heart open to Jesus' Lordship and life—that Peter will discover he *too* is the beloved disciple.

The difference in Peter and the Beloved Disciple is not that one is beloved and the other is not. The difference is that the unnamed disciple is learning to rest in and trust Jesus' love while Peter, ever restless and driven, is still trying to prove himself. He cannot quite believe he is *already* beloved (John 3:16). He doesn't realize that this side of Jesus' cross and resurrection, there is nothing left to prove. The gift of God's unconditional, inextinguishable love has already been given.

But there is hope for Peter, just as there is hope for me and for all who worry that they aren't good enough or special enough. The hope is that he, and I, and others like us will do as Jesus commands: take our eyes off everyone and everything else and go chasing after Jesus on the journey of discipleship. As we follow Jesus, we learn how precious he is and find the way to the life he makes possible. As we follow Jesus in the *Way* of discipleship, we discover the *Truth* that leads to the *Life* abundant and eternal he alone can give (14:6). Little wonder Jesus' first words to Peter, as well as his last, were "Follow *me*!" (Mark 1:16-17; John 1:40, 43; 21:2).

A while back, I shared in a pastoral conversation with a second grader about becoming a Christian. I was skeptical whether she grasped enough of the gospel to be baptized as a believer.

Still, I plowed on, explaining the meaning of the words "Lord" (9:38; 20:28) and "Savior" (4:42). "'Lord' means Jesus is the one brings God near," I explained. "And 'Lord' means Jesus is the one we follow. But there's another important part to being a Christian, and that is asking Jesus to be our Savior. 'Savior' means even when we don't follow Jesus like we should, he still loves and forgives us. So we live our lives trying to *follow Jesus* and asking *his forgiveness* when we don't."

"Oh, I get it," she volunteered. "It's like you're following Jesus through the woods. Then you bump into a tree and skin your knee. You fall down and start to cry. But then Jesus turns around, comes back and kisses your knee, and makes everything better."

My jaw dropped in surprise at her grasp of the gospel. "Exactly," I said, dumbfounded. "Exactly!"

Following Jesus in faith and longing is something a second grader can do. That means it is something *you* can do too. Today, as in first-century Palestine, Jesus' bold promise stands true: "I am the light of the world. The one who follows me will never walk in darkness but will have the light of life" (8:12)!

There is a reason the Beloved Disciple never identifies himself in the Gospel of John. It is because he knew he was but the first of many such disciples. Indeed, that is why he wrote his remarkable witness (20:31): so you too could experience and treasure the riveting, life-changing truth that *You* also are the beloved disciple!

"*Beloved*, we are God's children *now*; what we will be has not yet been revealed. What we do know is this: when [Christ] is revealed, we will be like him, for we will see him as he is!" (1 John 3:2).

Starting today, love, trust, and follow Jesus, for only then will you discover that you are beloved of God today, tomorrow, and forevermore.

Bibliography

The Access Bible, New Revised Standard Version with Apocrypha (paperback 9872A). New York: Oxford University Press, USA, 1999.

Barfield, James E. Photography by Walter G. Elliott. *Living Macon Style*. Macon GA: Indigo Custom Publishing, 2004.

Barclay, William. *The Gospel of John*. Volumes 1 and 2. Revised edition. Philadelphia: Westminster, 1975.

Brown, Raymond E. *The Anchor Bible: The Gospel According to John*. 2 volumes. Garden City NY: Doubleday & Company, Inc., 1981.

Kittel, G., and G. Friedrich, eds. *Theological Dictionary of the New Testament*. Translated by G. W. Bromiley. 10 vols. Grand Rapids: Eerdmans, 1964–1976.

Green, Michael. *Who Is This Jesus?* Nashville: Thomas Nelson Inc., 1992.

Griffith-Jones, Robin. *Four Witnesses*. San Francisco: Harper San Francisco, 2000.

Hull, William E. *John*. Volume 9 of the Broadman Bible Commentary. Nashville: Baptist Sunday School Board, 1971.

Jones, E. Stanley. *The Word Became Flesh*. New York: Abingdon Press, 1963.

Kysar, Robert. *John's Story of Jesus*. Minneapolis: Fortress Press, 1989.

Kreitzer, Larry. *The Gospel According to John.* Oxford: Regent's Park College, 1990.

The New Oxford Annotated Bible, New Revised Standard Version. New York: Oxford University Press, USA, 1991.

Quast, Kevin. *Reading the Gospel of John: An Introduction.* New York: Paulist Press, 1991.

Robertson, Archibald Thomas. *Word Pictures in the New Testament.* 6 volumes. Nashville: Broadman Press, 1930.

Setzer, Bob, Jr. *Christianity for Beginners.* Atlanta: Cooperative Baptist Fellowship, 1984.

Setzer, Robert B., Jr. *Encounters with the Living Christ: Meeting Jesus in the Gospel of John.* Valley Forge PA: Judson Press, 1999. Reprinted 2009.

Sloyan, Gerard S. *John.* Interpretation, a Bible Commentary for Teaching and Preaching. Atlanta: John Knox Press, 1988.

Stott, John R. W. *The Cross of Christ.* Downers Grove IL: Inter-Varsity Press, 1986.

Wright, N. T. *Surprised by Hope: Rethinking Heaven, the Resurrection, and the Mission of the Church.* New York: HarperOne, 2008.